RETREAT HANDBOOK

A-Way to Meaning

Virgil and Lynn Nelson

Judson Press • Valley Forge

RETREAT HANDBOOK

Copyright © 1976
Judson Press, Valley Forge, PA 19481

Unless otherwise indicated, Bible quotations in this volume are taken from *The Jerusalem Bible,* copyright © 1966 by Darton, Longman & Todd, Ltd. and Doubleday and Company, Inc. Used by permission of the publisher.

Bible quotations are also taken from the Revised Standard Version of the Bible, copyrighted 1952 and 1971 by the Division of Christian Education of the National Council of the Churches of Christ in the United States of America, and are used by permission.

Library of Congress Cataloging in Publication Data

Nelson, Virgil.
   Retreat handbook.

   Includes bibliographical references.
   1. Retreats—Handbooks, manuals, etc. I. Nelson, Lynn, joint author. II. Title.
BV5068.R4N44   269'.6'0202   75-23468
ISBN 0-8170-0694-X

Printed in the U.S.A.   ⊕

The photographs on pages 8, 42, 47, 48, 59, 63, 65, 74, and 75 are by Virgil Nelson, and on pages 36, 46, 49, 60, 73, 86, and 89 are by Rich Wagner.

Introduction

Retreats can be a powerful way to meaning. Living together with a specific purpose in an "away" place and time can bring forth spiritual growth, education, new perspective, deepened relationships, and renewal of strength and purpose in the life of the church fellowship.

In our twelve years of "retreating" and over one hundred retreats, we have found very few published guidelines for groups interested in the retreat planning process. Actual program ideas specifically designed for retreats are also scarce.

We hope that groups of many kinds with all levels of expertise can find useful resources in this manual. It covers the basics: *why* have a retreat, the nitty-gritties of *planning, executing,* and *evaluating* the retreat, and a wide variety of *resource materials* which have already been tried.

This handbook is possible only through the generous sharing of several hundred brothers and sisters who have made their ideas and resources available. We see it as the BEGINNING of a continuing process of sharing retreat materials, and we would appreciate your feedback and suggestions as to how the handbook could be more useful to you. We also hope to continue updating the materials and would appreciate copies of the retreat resources YOU have created.

Feedback and resources can be sent to us c/o Managing Editor, Judson Press, Valley Forge, PA 19481.

PEACE,
Virgil
&
Lynn

Acknowledgments

It is impossible to enumerate all the folk who have been (are) significant in our personal/spiritual growth, in developing the concepts in this manual, and in encouraging/supporting its formation.

Following are SOME of the persons contributing in the above three areas:

OUR THANKS TO:

our families, Ted and Jean, Fern and Violet, for their spirit of openness and joy toward ALL people and their willingness to include us in retreats and camping at an early age;

Robert Macoskey and other seminary profs who challenged me and encouraged my free association in type prior to organization and editing a final product;

those who worked with us in retreating/camping as co-directors, staff:

Carl Gittings, Bob Barnes, Larry Waltz, Wayne Murphy, Gordon Korb, Vince and Lib Siciliano, Larry Dobson, Tim and Ruth Peterson, Jim and Keitha Boardman, Richard and Carolyn Virgil, Don Wagner;

our co-workers with youth and young adults at Hatboro Baptist Church who learned with us and taught us:

Cushings, Cowperthwaites, Lockes, Blakes, Ewalds, Wilkersons, Porters, George Burke, Cleggs, Snaders, Rubischs, Rupples, MacGregors;

leaders among the youth themselves, some of whom are continuing in leadership positions:

Janet Barnett, Linda Ritchie, Rich Wagner, Ken Reed, Bob Trent, Tom Hudson, Tom Weaver, Barbara Burger, Barb and Joyce Hobensack, Val and Audrey Eisinger, Larry and Terry Jones, Danny Taylor, Bob Porter, Randy Stahl, Bill Kowprowsky, Mike and Doug Tilghman, Brad and Scott Jeffries, Nancy Reed, Nancy Trent;

the parents of the youth, the Board of Education, and the church fellowship who supported and encouraged ministry with all kinds of youth, both within and without the church;

Bill Stahl, our friend and colleague, whose trust and support continued even in the midst of confusion and our learning process;

Dennis Benson, who gave encouragement and valuable advice regarding the publication of this volume; the Howards and the Taylors, who gave time and creative energy in reviewing the manuscript and suggesting revisions; Harold Twiss, as managing editor, for his patience and valuable suggestions;

the WHOLE RE-CYCLE COMMUNITY and others who generously contributed their retreat material and ideas.

This is YOUR creation as well as ours!

Contents

Notes on the Use of This Manual

This manual is NO SUBSTITUTE FOR PLANNING. Putting together a retreat experience is fun, but it takes a lot of thinking and doing. It is easier if you have the right TOOLS and SUPPLIES. We hope you will find both in abundance.

WHEN YOU:

1. need some program ideas FAST:

   a. watch for the headings which interest you and dig in;

   b. sample actual retreat programs in Appendix (23–53. All items in the Appendix are designated by number and will be identified in the Manual as Appendix 5, etc.);

   c. look through the supplemental Program Ideas Chart;

   d. see quick planning possibilities (Appendix 2).

2. want to give more serious thought to the dimensions of retreating, curl up with the book for thorough reading.

3. start purchasing books and resources, check chapter 9 on resources and the List of Resources for a "starting list" of resource books for under $40; and a "grab-bag" list of materials.

4. want a checklist of things to consider when planning, go down the Table of Contents to remind yourself of areas you may have omitted.

Those who are new to retreating will find how and where to begin planning a retreat. Those who are experienced will find creative new program ideas and resources which have worked for others and new ways of viewing problems as REDEMPTIVE.

Section I
First Things First

OUR BASIC ASSUMPTIONS
about THE CHURCH
PEOPLE
RETREATS
GOD

1. Why Have a Retreat?

"It's a distraction from the ongoing work of the church."

"I have too many family and church responsibilities to take so much time out."

"The youth have the time, but retreats cost a lot of money."

"We've never done it before."

"Who is going to plan and lead the retreat?"

"We have enough trouble recruiting leadership."

"Who will teach Sunday School if all the teachers go on a retreat?"

The amount of TIME, ENERGY, AND MONEY involved in doing a retreat does distinguish it from other forms of gatherings for Christ. These elements are the basis not only for legitimate objections to retreats, but also for the retreat's UNIQUE contribution to the overall church program.

Retreating was a pattern common to Jesus and his disciples. As evidenced in the book of Mark, the disciples were heavily involved with people, and then they withdrew. For a time they were in the city; then they would head for the mountains or the wilderness or across the lake so they could be ALONE for prayer, teaching, reflection, and instruction.

In Mark 6:31 *(The Jerusalem Bible)* Jesus said to his disciples, "'You must come away to some lonely place all by yourselves and rest for a while,' for there were so many coming and going that the apostles had no time even to eat." They ended up having to go out in a boat to get away. Does this sound familiar: people being so busy, even with the Lord's work, that they are not able to care for their own needs?[1]

Jesus and his disciples withdrew for a purpose. The retreat is a TOOL and not an end in itself. The retreat form can extend the Body of Christ just as do gatherings in the form of committee meetings, classes, circles, worship services, and meals. Each is a different structure through which the Spirit of God may be expressed.

[1] Other Scripture references to retreating: Mark 1:12, Jesus going into the wilderness for forty days; Mark 1:35; 2:13; 3:7, 13; 4:1; 6:46-47; 9:2; 14:32.

Each of these forms may serve as a means for PEOPLE GATHERED to:

Praise   Prayer

GIVE GLORY TO GOD   Celebration

Stewardship   Thanksgiving

EXPERIENCE and SHARE   Salvation
Confession
Forgiveness
Healing
New Life
Chastening-Challenge   Freedom
Prophecy   L O V E
Action   Sacrificial Giving
Justice   Communion

The RETREAT in unique ways can zoom in on and expand any one of these functions of the living church:

The *longer time period* allows for:

G   C   C   sharing personal daily activities,
R   L   O
O   O   M   physical nearness in travel and tasks,
W   S   M
I   E   U   chances for both play and seriousness,
N   R   N
G   I   cumulative task sessions—   TRUST
    O
    N   DEPTH

The *need for advanced planning and additional resources* can INCREASE:

S	awareness of the importance of	OUR GROUP
T		FOR GOD,
E	renewal of dedication,	
W		
A	openness to gathering a wider range of resources	
R	(even outsiders) to apply to our task.	
D		
S		

Getting away to a *different environment* can provide the following benefits:

V H N — refreshment in natural beauty, relaxation,
I E E
S A W — a chance to stand back to get perspective,
I L — to perceive the overview and under-
O I L — currents, not just immediate crises,
N N I
  G F — a spur to tune in to the underlying issues,
    E

    a safe place to work through interpersonal and group problems,

    a chance for people to experiment with new behavior, discover new abilities.

THE SAME QUALITIES WHICH MAKE THE RETREAT AN ASSET TO CHURCH PROGRAMMING ARE THOSE WHICH REVEAL ITS LIMITATIONS.

Because the retreat form does take more time, resources, and energy than most other forms of church life, a group could unwittingly allow the retreat to become an end in itself if too many retreats were planned in a year. We have found that two to three weekend retreats a year for any one group is a reasonable taxing of the group's energy without interfering with the ongoing purposes of the group. Some groups do more. You and your group will discover your own balance.

The advantage of building close fellowship through retreats is precisely what may become a source of division in the larger church body. Closeness among group members is fine as long as it does not become exclusive. Retreat goers need to return with a spirit of openness and kinship with the other members of the church body. Attention to communication both before and after the retreat as to the purposes and accomplishments will strengthen the ties between groups.

The better the retreat in yielding peak experiences, the more it may "spoil" retreaters for dealing with reality back home. Exhilarated retreat goers feel a shock when they return to people who may be less committed, who are working less closely together with more frustration and less vision.

The reaction to a successful retreat may be, "Quick, let's go on another retreat!" The retreat then becomes a way of *escape* from the needed love-work of freeing the ongoing group life to meet more of the needs of the people, to be more expressive of Christ.

Despite these potential problems with retreating, we and many others have seen retreats play a very special part in church ministry. Annual church planning retreats, board retreats, choir retreats, family camping retreats, spiritual renewal retreats, as well as all kinds of retreats for youth are happening all across the country. One church uses the retreat form every six to eight weeks in place of the weekly high school church school classes.

The POWER of concentrated time, resources, and a special setting for:

1. stimulating personal spiritual growth,
2. deepening bonds between persons,
3. extending the Body of Christ in action

                    IS REAL!

Let's learn to utilize better this particularly fine vehicle for glorifying God.

2.   Whose Retreat?

Is it the church's? Is it the camp's?

Is it the leaders'? Or the participants'?

Is it the minister's? Or the board's?

Is it yours? Is it mine?

WE ASSUME THAT THE RETREAT BELONGS TO ALL THE PARTICIPANTS.

> Participants feel like they own the retreat when they are involved in the planning and implementing. See chapter 4.

Who are the retreat participants? They may include Christians and non-Christians—each of us is God's creation. We believe these things about each person (including leaders) on any retreat:

Amidst the reality of one's sin   NEGATIVITY
   laziness
   passivity   expecting entertainment
   consuming-nature   fear
                                 SELF-centeredness

SMALLness   AGGRESSIVEness

GOD'S SPIRIT CAN CALL FORTH IN EACH   JOY
           CREATIVITY   love

   ENERGY   initiative   risk taking

Ability to give and receive forgiveness

We EXPECT new creations in Christ to be emerging from the cracks and crannies, the smallnesses and mistakes, the petty power struggles and self-indulgences because WE ALSO EXPECT THE HOLY SPIRIT TO BE WITH US.

If we take the Holy Spirit seriously, we can be less uptight about mistakes and imperfections, for there is the possibility of healing, learning, and redemption in every crisis or pitfall.

Taking the Holy Spirit seriously frees the planners and doers from *overplanning*. We no longer need to attempt to anticipate and rigidly control each step of the retreat. Innovations of the Spirit are invited!

Taking the Holy Spirit seriously means that we will not *underplan.* God is not our cosmic bellhop who will save any and all situations for which we are unprepared. Underplanning can mean that we do not care about what happens to the persons who are on the retreat.

Taking the Holy Spirit seriously reminds us all

that we are   children of God,
                sinners and forgiven,
                            brothers   and   sisters   in
                                                Christ.
This awareness opens us to one another in new and deeper ways.

We assume also that the presence of the Holy Spirit can make sacred any activity or situation feeling his TOUCH. Hence we do not make rigid distinctions between "sacred" and "secular" activities on the retreat.

ALL ACTIVITIES ARE POTENTIALLY SACRED. People came from miles to be with Brother Lawrence who was washing pots and pans because God was present with him in THAT activity.   God's activity is not
                    confined to:

                    small-group Bible studies,
                    worship services,
                    prayer time.

We might find him:

        whispering with us in the cabin,
        in a water-balloon fight,
        in sweeping the kitchen,
        in hassles over curriculum,
        in a joke.

God is present not only in the midst of everydayness but also in the problems or crises which happen. A discussion of how some specific problem incidents have been TRANSFORMED through God's love can be found in chapter 23.

Let us meet each aspect of our retreat preparation and action expecting to find God in us and in all his creation.

3. Two Case Histories: Success and Disaster

RETREAT SUCCESS

The group members were looking forward to returning to their favorite place in the Pocono Mountains to recapture the feeling of group unity.

However, the group planning for this senior high youth fellowship outing had a rough time, for there was little agreement on the purpose of the retreat and as a result, there was a feeling of futility. Therefore, the adult leaders took a more directive role than usual to plan a structure to help the group deal with its problems of low trust and commitment.

Twenty-four youth and five adults gathered at the church on Friday evening to leave for the retreat. There was some excitement at the prospect of getting away and of having an all-night marathon session.

The night turned out to be hard work. The leaders had provided a number of participational exercises to guide the exploration of trust in the group, trust in oneself, and trust in God. Disagreements emerged as the group began a physical sociogram which was highly threatening. A deeper level of honest feedback arose from the conflict, and the structure planned was discarded in favor of the spontaneity of the sharing begun. As the hours passed, the mood moved from urgent self-defense to acceptance of one another's needs and desires, to group hilarity, and to exhaustion and sleep.

Saturday had been planned as a day of regrouping and refreshment with free time, planned group recreation, and light spiritual input via films. Preparation of meals by small groups provided opportunities for building the spirit of cooperation and sharing.

Sunday morning people were ready to dig in to study the Word, express themselves, and make new commitments. Through guided personal tasks, small-group dramatic interpretation of three Scripture passages, a short presentation on the biblical meaning of covenant, and creation of their own group covenant, all the participants were drawn in and searched their own relationship to God and to the group. As silence spread in the group, wind blew into the room, lifting the pages of the new covenant. No other breeze was felt that day. The

worship had lasted three and one-half hours. Years later many remembered this experience marked by the unexpected wind as a very close experience with God.

Why was the retreat a success? Some of the key factors seem to have been:

1. The planning group did not fool itself by wishful thinking; it recognized the group as being less than ideal and identified the group needs (for heightened trust, commitment, and unity). It planned schedule and program elements with these needs in mind.
2. The leaders were open to changes of schedule during the retreat in response to people's needs and God's direction.
3. Some retreaters went expectant of change, ready to work, to listen, and to pray. They were catalysts for others.

The extent of reconciliation brought about through the vehicle of this retreat amazed everyone. The group had turned around. The breeze freshening the air in the room symbolized the group experiencing a fresh start with a deeper commitment to follow Jesus.

(For more details of program and schedule for this retreat see Appendix 41.)

RETREAT DISASTER

Everyone was looking forward to a terrific shore weekend retreat like last summer's.

The senior high youth fellowship wasn't quite the same—there were some new people in the group and some of the neat people from the last year would not be there. Nevertheless, the marvelous fun and spirit would be experienced once again!

Reservations were made at the same private campground. One youth took care of the correspondence, paid a deposit, and received a letter of confirmation well in advance. The camp managers needed to know how many were coming; so registration was begun early. Since one of the goals of the retreat was to overcome some of the hassles between group members and to develop more unanimity of spirit, the youth decided that only group members could go on the retreat. A registration deadline was established. One person was designated to take the registrations and money.

Other purposes for the retreat were decided: to have fun and to experience the presence of God.

Committees were set up: food, program, and schedule. Two planning meetings were held in homes. Resources were gathered. Leaders and rides were lined up.

Friday came. Six adult leaders and thirty youth were off to the shore.

THE WEEKEND WAS A DISASTER!
WHY?

What went wrong?

When the group arrived at the camp, the manager claimed that the camp was full and refused to accommodate the group even though they had their confirmation. They finally arranged for the group to stay at another camp nearby. The resultant anger, disappointment, and the late-night tent pitching could well have been transformed into a new adventure had there not been more serious BASIC problems involved in the preparation for the retreat.

Mistakes were made in planning and in the handling of leadership needs that created a crisis *before* the group even left the church parking lot.

Mistakes in planning

1. The decision about "Who could go" was NOT explored thoroughly enough by group members. Some were dissatisfied that their boyfriends (girlfriends) who did not belong to the group were not allowed to go. (The president of the group decided at the last minute not to go because her guy could not come.)
2. The registration deadline was not clear to all.
3. Because it was unclear as to who was to line up transportation, some of the youth recruited friends "outside" the group to drive. A leader had recruited several adult drivers who were also to serve as leaders although they had not had previous contact with the group. Hence the PARKING LOT CRISIS: Who should be sent home? Should they send back the youth who were ready to drive (but were not group members) or the last-minute adult leadership? What was fair? NONE OF THESE DRIVERS HAD REGISTERED. A leader decided that the adult drivers could go but not the youth drivers. This made friends of the non-group members angry. The youth with cars solved their problem by following the group to the shore and camping in a neighboring campsite, so

that the question as to whether they were retreat participants persisted.

4. The small planning committees did not include the strong social leaders. Even though the committees reported plans for schedule and program back to the whole group, little discussion and therefore little commitment or ownership emerged from others in the group. The food committee members felt used when *few* pitched in to help make the meals, but *many* felt free to criticize the soggy spaghetti.
5. In the program planning, the committee did not take into account realistic expectations of people being asked to implement the program. For example: *(a)* Some musicians in the group were lined up to lead group singing. However, the musicians preferred to perform. *(b)* Those given speaking, prayer, and reading leadership responsibilities had "small" voices and a lack of leadership confidence.
6. Major ground rules were reviewed, but minor ground rules were not made clear and agreed to by all.
7. Last-minute recruitment of leaders, little clarification of the division of labor, and no time for communication prior to the retreat contributed to an adult leadership crisis, compounding the above.

Problems in adult leadership

1. Due to last-minute recruitment, three leaders had not been in on the planning. One was not aware of the ground rules and violated one.
2. The exhaustion of the adult couple which sponsored the group and their very late arrival at the campsite rendered them less functional. They did not participate in several important activities.
3. The adult who had usually taken ultimate responsibility was not along, and no one else wanted the responsibility. Hence, the woman who ended up taking this responsibility resisted doing it, felt uncomfortable, and became rigid. She was not open to the human needs and the flickering of the Holy Spirit which might have altered the schedule.

Results

Weak programs. Those few who planned did most of the implementing with little spirit of cooperation from others. The director ended up dragging reluctant leaders and youth from sleeping bags to a sunrise service on the beach where the sun could not be seen nor voices heard above the sound of waves.

For once, no one minded leaving the retreat to go home. Aggravations and unresolved conflicts and disap-

SGT. STRIPES . . . FOREVER

by Bill Howrilla

Reprinted by permission of Newspaper Enterprise Association (or NEA).

pointments were high. "Let's forget the whole thing " was a frequent comment.

Evaluation of the retreat was painful. With the help of an adult leader who had not been on the retreat (hence was more emotionally neutral) the solutions to the leadership problems at both youth and adult levels emerged, and over a period of time the leaders developed.

The retreat had kicked the complacency out of everyone. The need to take people's needs and abilities more seriously was imperative.

THE RETREAT WAS A DISASTER, but it became
PART OF THE ROAD TO
        GROUP   RENEWAL   AND
                STRENGTH.

Disasters, when learned from, can be redemptive experiences, although they are not necessarily so. Such an extreme problem situation as that above can be prevented by

        GOOD PLANNING,
        GOOD LEADERSHIP,
        GOOD UTILIZATION OF EVALUATION.

                        Read on.

Section II
Perspectives

The Process of Planning
The Process of Learning

Let us meet each aspect of our retreat preparation and action expecting to find God in us and in all of his creation!

4.   The Process of Planning

Many of the ideas in this section are just plain common sense. However, we have found that people sometimes need help in applying their knowledge from one field to another.

Planning a retreat is like planning any other event. It entails forethought about who is involved; what are the needs, wishes, and resources; what are the most important goals; what needs to be done in what order to accomplish the goals; then action; and finally evaluation.

There are several resource manuals which describe more fully what is involved in good planning:

Broholm, Richard R., *Strategic Planning for Church Organizations*. Valley Forge: Judson Press, 1969.

"Steps in Program Planning," developed by the Episcopal Church; distributed by the United Church of Christ, Central Distribution Service, P.O. Box 7286, St. Louis, MO 65177

"Leader-in-the-Box," resource kit on Creative Problem Solving (3 cassettes, 6 posters, 7 participant's books), available at Judson Book Stores; $24.95.

Carroll, John L., and Ignatius, Keith L., *Youth Ministry: Sunday, Monday, and Every Day*. Valley Forge: Judson Press, 1972.

Simply summarized GOOD PLANNING:

starts with	EVALUATION—gathering facts and analyzing the data according to needs and values
derives	statement of GOALS for future
develops	general plan—STRATEGY
breaks down	procedural steps—TACTICS
risks	ACTION
then does	EVALUATION

See also Appendix 1.

For tactics on how to get started in your retreat planning, see the chapters in Section III: "How to Do It," particularly chapter 7 on Goal Setting. This chapter is focused upon the whys and hows of the planning process as such.

WHY PLAN?

Planning is a means to get what we want. Of course all roads lead to where we are going if we do not know where we are going. Hence, one of the most important aspects of planning is identifying and clarifying what we want to happen—GOAL SETTING.

Once we know our goals, planning is a means:

to make available resources and equipment needed for efficient action toward our goals,

to sequence activity so that it adds up to a larger accomplishment,

to apply our principles of operation consistently throughout the activity.

WHY PLAN?
IT'S PRACTICAL

Joseph, in Genesis 41, created a fourteen-year plan to deal with the famine: seven years of collection and storage during the time of plenty and then seven years of distribution and sales.

Moses, in Exodus 18:13-27, was persuaded by his father-in-law to recruit and train leaders to help him more fully accomplish his goal of dispensing justice.

Planning indicates caring enough about the people and the event to do some thinking and activity beforehand to make it more likely that the event will come to pass and will accomplish its purpose.

Not all planning works.

Under-planning results in confusion, inefficiency, extra work, frustration, and insecurity. (Walk in Joseph's brothers' shoes.)

Over-planning can also occur. (In Matthew 6 Jesus tells us not to worry excessively about the morrow or about our provisions, to seek first the kingdom of God.) Over-planning can squeeze out God. In a rigid, packed schedule or with a leader who has to be in control of every event there is little room for creativity and growth as individuals and as a group, little room for Holy Spirit action.

Good plans are a BALANCE of TRUST and CARING: trust in God's leading and in his expression through people, and enough care to
prepare the field,
set a course,
and keep the faith!

PLAN WHAT?

What specifically is planned for the retreat ideally depends on the goals which are set. The general things that need to be planned for any retreat include:

Creating a planning task force
Goal setting
Planning the program
Resource gathering
Creating the schedule
Developing ground rules
Recruiting and training leadership
Arranging for facilities
Arranging for meals
Handling registration
Promoting
Budgeting
Fund raising
Arranging transportation
Handling and preventing rumors
Arranging for insurance
Evaluating

Each of these tasks is important to the outcome of the retreat although some may seem more visible and central than others. (See the case history of a disaster, in chapter 3, for an illustration of the importance of many of these task areas.)

It is hoped that the decisions which are made in each of these WHAT areas reflect the goals first set.

What things need to be planned and what can be left to the resourcefulness of the people on the spot? We have found that some decision making before the retreat is helpful in each of the seventeen areas listed above. During the retreat, opportunities may present themselves to expand, extend, and even revise and change some of these areas if we are neither so in love with our plan that we cannot change, nor so lacking in faith that we do not trust innovations.

WHAT we plan with God's guidance may then be a framework to be filled out by God working in us during the retreat.

WHO PLANS?

Planning can be done by one, three, or fifty people; by leaders, small committees, large committees or groups as a whole; by people aged 8 or 108.

Who does the planning and how the planning is done depend upon some *group givens*:

Who Is in the Group?

How many people are in the group? Is the group shrinking, growing, or stable?

What are the ages; how wide is the age span?

Do people know each other?

How many personal or interpersonal hassles are there?

How many people have leadership experience and ability?

Is there anyone who has helped plan a retreat before?

What are the attitudes toward authority?

What decision-making style is preferred by leaders, by participants?

How many different cultures are represented in the group?

What Has the Group Experienced in the Past?

How long has the group existed?

Is there continuity provided by leaders despite change in group membership over a period of time?

What kinds of leadership style(s) have there been?

What have been the group's purposes?

Has the group been on a retreat or planned one before?

What Does the Group Want to Be Like in the Future?

Are people satisfied with size, decision-making style, and activity?

Do they want change in any of these areas?

Because practice in planning is useful in developing leaders, people, and groups, as many people as possible should be involved in planning.

Staging the Sharing of Responsibility. The following list starts with the tasks which are easiest for inexperienced people to handle and moves to those which require more complex skills:

Require more commonly used communication and mechanical skills	1. Arranging for location, facility, and meals 2. Arranging for transportation 3. Promoting 4. Fund raising 5. Registration
Require more complex communication and action skills and clear understanding of goals	6. Creating a planning task force 7. Arranging for meals when group will be doing own cooking 8. Discussing ground rules 9. Checking insurance 10. Rumor prevention 11. Recruiting leadership 12. Budgeting
Require ability to think abstractly, to consider relationship between content and process, less concrete measuring posts, more complex human-relationship skills.	13. Deciding on goals 14. Transitioning between goals and specific ways to implement them in program and schedule 15. Leadership training

REMINDER! This is not the order in which the tasks should be done. Goal setting is among the first when possible. This is the *order of difficulty* of the tasks.

In deciding who plans what, it is also helpful to recognize that some of these tasks are rather mechanical in nature while others appear to be more central to the shape of the retreat. More people will want to have a voice in deciding the location, the theme (goals, program, and schedule), the ground rules, and who can go. The other tasks are more supportive in nature and do not necessarily

require the involvement of many in the group. However, the importance of the task is not to be judged by the number of people involved. Any one of the above planning tasks can have far-reaching effects on the retreat. (Note the case history of disaster.)

Who does the retreat *planning* may not at all be *who* does the *implementing* of those plans during the retreat. This division of labor is most apparent when people from outside the group have been asked to take the major responsibility for leadership during the retreat. Also in youth retreating, we have found that although young people may grow to be capable of the entire retreat planning, they are usually not capable—due to emotional immaturity and short-life experience—to handle the full leadership needs of carrying out their retreat. Those who have participated in the planning *do* have specific knowledge and an emotional investment which equip them to be good coordinators for implementation on the retreat. Other group members and outside specialists can work with them to share in the labor.

WHOSE RETREAT? Who *plans* influences who *owns* the retreat. How many people have been left out? Has the Holy Spirit been listened to in the busyness of the planning meetings?

WHEN PLAN?

Let's hope that you do not wait until after the guests arrive to plan your meal!

It is obvious that when you are planning a fairly complex activity, you need to put some time and energy in *ahead of time* to ensure that it runs smoothly once the activity is started.

The lead-time one needs to start planning in advance of the retreat varies according to how dependent the group is on outside resources. For example:

1. Obtaining an outside resource person for program leadership takes the time of deciding who, writing letters, and arranging for expenses, transportation, and meeting place. Inviting the leader may need to be done six months to a year ahead of time if the resource person is in demand.

2. The group might need to contact and reserve lodging and meals well in advance (sometimes more than a year).

When the group is "doing it itself"—creating and carrying out its own program and meals—more time closer to the event will be required with two to three time-consuming work sessions.

Generally, the more complex the retreat—

the longer the distance or duration,

the more people anticipated,
the more varied the groups involved—

the more time is needed in various aspects of planning (possibly for fund raising, more attention to transportation details, or more complex scheduling and programming). It is obvious that an overnight retreat in the church is simpler in elements of location, transportation, insurance, and expense and therefore could take far less planning time than would be required by a week-long trip to another state. A three-week trip out of the country might take two years in planning. (See Appendix 2 for Quick Planning Possibilities.)

Most of the planning needs to be done BEFORE the retreat event. The elements which seem most possible to plan during the retreat are: some division of labor among leaders and group members for implementing the schedule, program, and maintenance; some program development (if resources have been gathered); and some decisions on recreation activities. Often, discussion of ground rules is left until then; we have found that this delay can be trouble producing. (See Retreat Disaster, chapter 3.)

Evaluation may be done during or after the retreat event. We have found it helpful to do evaluation at both times. A more systematic and thorough job is likely to be done after the retreat, for there is more willingness to look at the retreat objectively with some perspective in time, especially if the retreat was a highly emotional experience (either high or low). Evaluation upon return home also helps to incorporate learnings of the retreat into the ongoing group life back home.

A rushed planning job may leave out the time needed to be attentive to the real needs of God's creatures and his will for us. Just a word of caution, then: allow a little extra time for listening.

WHERE PLAN?

If several people in the group are involved in the planning, where the planning is done can make a difference.

We have found that holding several small-group meetings scheduled in between regular meeting times works effectively in getting the nitty-gritty of the planning work done, then to be presented for review, evaluation, and decision making by the group as a whole. When most of the planning for the retreat is done in the regular group meetings, especially if done as a committee of the whole instead of in small planning groups, the retreat can get "old" before it even occurs.

Have the planning meetings in homes or a place other than the regular meeting place! The new location can give the small groups a sense of the special significance of their planning tasks.

For a long, large, or complex retreat a small planning retreat might be in order, USE A RETREAT TO PLAN A RETREAT. Then all of the values of the retreat form go to enhance the planning process!

WHAT   WHERE

WHO   WHEN

HOW
we plan
reflects

WHY
we plan.

If we care about the value of persons and the life-giving power of Christ, our planning process will show it. Opportunities for personal growth, inspiration, service, and learning are all present in the activity of planning. The foregoing tips may help so that we do not cheat ourselves and others out of this opportunity for
ENCOUNTERING GOD.

5. The Process of Learning

Good News! People of all ages *can* change. All are forgiven and freed of the past and may start new through the Way of Jesus!

HOW PEOPLE GROW AND CHANGE

How do we best encourage and edify each other as we learn to walk in His footsteps?

People change in different ways:

- Saul changed to Paul in a dramatic overnight intervention.
- Doubting Thomas needed to see and feel tangibles.
- The disciples needed to live and work together in the presence and guidance of their Leader in order to learn about loving God and their neighbors. Even then, they at times fell back to old ways.

Too often in the church people have assumed that attitudinal changes come primarily through the rational thinking process (for example, that it is sufficient to inform people of the Good News and the new life-style). This is the usual way we have attempted to change attitudes in society also: "If people only knew the facts (about smoking, racism, poverty), they would change their attitudes and behavior." The FACTS DO influence change, but new information is only one of the forces needed.

Human behavior is also partly rooted in emotions. If we are to change our behavior, these feelings must be dealt with. If our goal involves a change of attitude or action, then we will anticipate a higher incidence of change if the means used is expressive or experiential. PRACTICE, in symbolic ways through exercises, games, or simulations or in the actual situation, with the presence of brothers and sisters in Christ to guide, is an effective way to try on new behavior and to explore issues of valuing.

There are several ways in which values are transmitted:

1. MORALIZING (Authoritarian style)

Telling, preaching, evangelizing, words with authority and fervor from a person vested with power.

PROS: Efficient in time and energy.

Summarizes learning and wisdom from the past.
Can protect people from painful mistakes.

CONS: More than one authority (school, parents, church, Bible, science, business, society), so there are many conflicting messages which can result in confusion or drop-out.
May influence *words* and not actions—people saying one thing, living another; church on Sunday, hell the rest of the week.

2. LAISSEZ-FAIRE

No general rule applying to all; each has own and "does his own thing"; trial-and-error method.

PROS: Gives individuals room to experiment to find out for themselves what they value.
Acknowledges the variety of human experience.
Emphasizes ability to choose.

CONS: Leaves people open to all ranges of mistakes and painful or destructive consequences. May be overwhelming.
Takes into account little learning of others from past experience.
Inefficient in time, energy; costly in human lives and spirits.
Increase in conflict versus cooperation.

3. MODELING

Person attractive or vested with authority demonstrating by behavior (as well as words) his/her values.

PROS: A good model, where behavior is consistent with words and consistent with God, can powerfully transmit a life-style to COPY. Shows how it works.
Tends to influence a person's ACTIONS not just his/her outer shell.

CONS: There may be many models demonstrating

conflicting value systems (among peers AND leaders) resulting in confusion. (Parents or others who don't want that certain "bad element" in their group or their child's are giving credit to the power of modeling for change in values.)

Less staying power—one's loyalty to an idol or model can change (even be fickle) because it is often based on a feeling of attraction (charisma). Values are not one's own but emulated, tried on, perhaps to be discarded later.

4. VALUES-CLARIFICATION approach [1]

A process of guided experiential learning for identifying values and beliefs, examining behavior in light of them and alternative values, and selecting values to incorporate into own system.

PROS: The opportunity for an individual to make one's own choices and evaluate consequences of own behavior enhances ownership of value system.

Provides a structure for people to sort out alternatives and look at the amount of harmony between their beliefs, values, and actions.

Eliminates need for "policing." Instead offers guide to help with "facing-up."

CONS: Takes a lot of time and energy.

The approach is a neutral tool which could be used to clarify any value system; not necessarily Christian in orientation.

It is risky. Participant might get hurt.

It is painful to stand by and watch people make mistakes; our tendency is to want to bail people out of trouble (and perhaps out of learning).

Demands some maturity and communication skills of participants and guides.

It seems to us that Jesus used the moralizing, modeling, and values-clarification approaches. We feel, then, that it is important for all three forces to be available for guiding people in church activities so that individuals may grow in responsibility before God for their values, goals, and lifestyle.

So, in this journey of learning it is helpful to have some good guides.

[1] See Sidney B. Simon, *et al., Values Clarification* (New York: Hart Publishing Company, Inc., 1972).

QUALITIES OF GOOD GUIDES

Everyone has some gifts of the Spirit. No gift is better than another; all are part of the Body. (See Ephesians 4.)

Jesus said that God will perform through you and me the same works that he performed and even GREATER ones! (See John 14:12.)

You may have gifts you have not yet discovered. Jesus chose the common folk to be his followers and TRAINED them to be disciples. We can learn to be disciples. All of us have potential to be guides to some people, and all of us need to be guided by others.

A LEADER is any person who is respected by the group for his/her particular characteristics, attitudes, or skills, or for his/her willingness to assume responsibility for particular functions.

There are many varied *leadership styles.* Leaders or guides give varying amounts of power for decision making to the group members.

All decision-making styles fit somewhere in the range between

AUTHORITARIAN ——————— LAISSEZ-FAIRE
(The will of one person   (Each group member
structures the group)   does own thing)

THERE ARE HEALTHY GROUPS ALL ALONG
THIS CONTINUUM.

(Where does your group fit?)

There may be times in a group's life when one style is more appropriate than another.

The *Authoritarian* style is more appropriate when:

1. The group members are floundering, unable to organize themselves, not knowing what they want or how to accomplish goals.
2. The group is in early stages of formation, and someone needs to convene the group and to provide cohesive power for gathering strangers.
3. The group is in transition and some external structure is needed to ensure continuity and to maximize cohesion.
4. A major crisis has occurred where immediate decision making and action are crucial.
5. People are gathering for only a short period of time for a specific task.
6. The leader experiences himself/herself as a child of God and therefore:
   - does not need to influence the group for own feeling of self-worth
   - is able to let go of power when the group is ready

to take more responsibility. He/she may even choose to use authority to develop this readiness for shared leadership.

7. The leader is outstanding in vision, talent, and charisma, and the group gathers in response. (Healthy as long as the content of the leader's vision and the means are not contrary to Christ's spirit.)

The *Laissez-faire* style is more appropriate when:

1. No one is recognized as the authority, and people are gathering for what help they can give one another.
2. People are coming together for play or friendship or self-renewal.
3. The group members are less interested in achieving something than in being together.
4. People are comfortable with an unpredictable happening.
5. Each person is willing to take responsibility for himself or herself, make own decisions, develop own preferences.
6. No individual's action frequently overrides another's freedom or threatens the legal basis for the group's continuing existence.

There are advantages and disadvantages in each decision-making style. When the conditions outlined above are not present, either extreme becomes painful.

When there are wide differences in individual preferences for decision-making style in the same group, a great deal of tension occurs. Such conflict can be challenging and conducive to Christian growth if the group values spending time exploring the feelings involved. However, if the group wants to proceed with its other goals, the best resolution may be for the group to divide so that each part can then function in the style it prefers.

A decision-making model that can slide from the middle of the continuum toward either extreme can be called *Enabled Participation*. The leader functions as a group member at times and as a catalyst, resource person, and adviser (enabler) at other times. The group members take varying degrees of responsibility for decision making and implementation.

Comparatively, the Enabled Participation model has a more complex structure of relationships than either of the extremes and so is perhaps more difficult to maintain. But it has the value of allowing for the most positive qualities of both extremes: for the personal responsibility and creative risk taking maximized in the Laissez-Faire form and for the organized efficiency and group cohesion maximized in the Authoritarian form.

The middle range of the *Enabled-Participation* style is appropriate in group life when:

1. The group members have some ideas about goals and how to accomplish them.
2. The group members recognize when they are unable to do what they want and ask for the help of a specially skilled person.
3. Some individual group members are willing to take coordinating and leadership responsibility.
4. Some group members have the capability of carrying out tasks required to meet goals.
5. The group is having conflicts among members and wants extra help to deal with the problem.
6. The group wants to get out of a rut.
7. The enabler is aware of the dual nature of his/her role and is constantly reflecting on the appropriateness of his/her participation at the time.
8. Group members and/or the enabler are sensitive to the potential for the possibility of subtle manipulation under the guise of "enabling" and have the strength to challenge this behavior.

This model seems to be more consistent than the others with the assumption that people who are "new creations in Christ" are free, because of God's love, to reach out and risk, to interact and care, to join together to be an effective Body for Christ, not to be isolated either by rules (Authoritarian form) or indifference (Laissez-faire form). Each group member can increasingly enjoy and dare to express his or her own "gifts of the Spirit," taking responsibility for self and others and yet being open to ask and trust for help and healing when it is needed.

The Enabled-Participation style is ACHIEVABLE. We have found that a group functioning at either extreme and inexperienced in retreat planning can move toward the participatory style. Group members can learn to take responsibility for the entire retreat-planning process (with the exception of the area of leadership training which takes more complex skills) over a period of two years or six retreats. Staging the sharing of responsibility is the method of this transition. (See p. 18).

 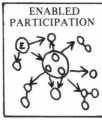 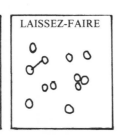

AUTHORITARIAN   ENABLED PARTICIPATION   LAISSEZ-FAIRE

Whatever leadership style you prefer, guides and leaders are looked to as *models* of aspects of the Christian life-style. Leaders are noticed not just in their area of specific responsibility but at other times—when relaxing, eating, etc. During the retreat, are the leaders showing that they care for themselves and others by their own pace and schedule? Does the leader take time to be a real person with his or her spouse or is the partner taken for granted? Other participants—especially youth who are experimenting with intimacy—as well as the spouse will

quickly get the message communicated by such actions.

Superhuman dedication and energy investments are too often required from leaders, especially on youth retreats. Having sufficient staff can help. Also, if leaders recognize their own potential power as models, they may be willing to pay more attention to their own life-style during the retreat and bring it into closer harmony with their stated beliefs and values.

Good guides take time to TUNE IN.

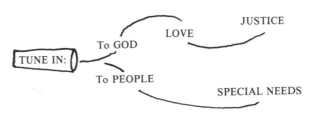

Communication depends in part on a well-functioning *receiver*. Listening helps us to time our sharing for the optimum learning moments of others. Every situation is pregnant with possibilities to learn about meaning in life. "Have you eyes that do not see, ears that do not hear?"

Activities (even free-time activities) can be painful to some; be alert for those teachable moments.

What the leaders send out in the way of *nonverbal signals* also matters.

Expectations can be felt.

Double messages are experienced as confusion. People seem to grow best when they are expected to live up to their potential and accepted when they don't. Most often people sense when they are respected and trusted, and they respond by being trustworthy. Leaders' fears may breed further mistrust and may influence people to fulfill the reputation expected. Anyone set on proving that

someone or some group is bad will probably get ample "proof."

Leaders may reasonably expect some testing and experimenting behavior among youth. There may be adults who have reputations as gripers or shafters. What actually occurs is to a large extent influenced by your attitude, your expectations of the group and individuals.

WINTHROP   **by Dick Cavalli**

Reprinted by permission of Newspaper Enterprise Association (or NEA).

LOVE People grow when cared for, affirmed, counted as worthwhile. The Lord chose to be reconciled to us people while we were still sinners, and his LOVE-ACTION frees us to be "new creations." May this healing, change-producing love flow through us as retreat leaders. (For another listing of characteristics of leaders, see Appendix 47.)

GUIDES WITH YOUTH[2]

Adults working with youth need:

1. to be personally stable.
2. to have at least average self-confidence and skills.
3. to have a high capacity for openness, love, and acceptance of others.
4. to be honest, reasonable, fair, firm, consistent with known limits of tolerance and patience.
5. to have fairly high tolerance for noise and seeming disorder.
6. to be willing to share their own growth process, questions, and pains.
7. to be willing to struggle through some hard spots.
8. to have some playfulness.
9. to be committed yet open-minded.

[2] For an excellent discussion about "adult-sharers," see "A Junior-High Potpourri," Bernard C. Linnartz, *Strategy,* March–May, 1974.

LEADERS CAN GROW

Leaders don't have to be perfect! With some guidance, they, too, can grow.

You may not have time for specific leadership-development training before each retreat; but in the process of planning and carrying out the event, the designated leaders can try on new responsibilities and attitudes with support and guidance.

Some suggestions about tools to stimulate growth in leaders' awareness and skills follow. You may want to include some whenever you ordinarily get together or plan a special training event.

1. Spend time in PRAYER and MEDITATION.

If you are not relaxed, at ease, centered, you cannot hear the will of God. Thousands of stimuli hit us every minute. The choices required of us as guides mean we need a measuring rod.

Study the Word.

Pray conversational or historical prayers (especially appropriate for leaders): Serenity Prayer and the prayer of St. Francis of Assisi.

Ask for one another's support.

Be ready to give and receive healing love.

2. READ or discuss books and articles about communication:

- Basic principles of Transactional Analysis. Easy to understand communication theory. Good beginning books: Muriel James's *Born to Love, Born to Win.* (See list of resources.) Practice analyzing different communication statements: Was the parent speaking? The child or the adult? Who answered? Were the communications mixed? Discuss: life-positions, transactions, crossed transactions, games, life-scripts, strokes. Relate the retreating.
- *Parent Effectiveness Training,* by Thomas Gordon.
- See List of Resources.

3. PRACTICE handling problems.

Discuss and role-play actual handling of specific problems while the pressure is OFF! Practice seeing them as "teachable moments."

Possible Teachable Moments
(1) in time of conflict, (2) when there is a feeling of inadequacy, (3) when a need or problem is recognized, (4) when a goal is set, and (5) when a person is searching for meaning in life.[3]

Some teachable moments are planned; some happen spontaneously; some are dreaded. They may involve any combination of participants and leaders. No one is exempt.

EXAMPLE for role play:
With the group of leaders, role-play a counselor discovering three senior high boys in the cabin reading *Playboy.*

How can this situation become a teachable moment?

What if the first statement is "Put that away!" or "Let me have that! Christians don't read that trash!" Using the TA model, that was a parental statement. It often leads to a power struggle hooking various argumentative (child) statements.

What might be some opening adult statements which

[3] Martha M. Leypoldt, *Learning Is Change* (Valley Forge: Judson Press, 1971), p. 59.

could be the basis for values clarification and reflection by the youth on the pros and cons of their choice of reading matter?

"Some good cartoons in there, huh? Of course you can't ignore the pictures. What do you enjoy about the magazine?" These openers can lead into serious discussion about the place and meaning of sex in relationships, the plastic portrayal of women and their disposable qualities as portrayed by *Playboy,* the biblical understanding of the body, sex.

(Such an approach may be very HARD, especially when you experience strong negative feelings. It may take practice to express our feelings in a way which fosters further communication rather than shutting the door.)

The conditions for change and growth on the part of leaders seem to be the same as those for other folks:
an anchor of faith;
the stimulation of challenges, problems, new information, and tools;
models;
the support of fellow pilgrims;
and a chance to practice.

Section III
How to Do It

Friends, as you read the following suggestions for planning a retreat, do not feel that you have to perfect ALL of them before your next retreat! Build from what you've already been doing in planning, adding a couple of new dimensions at a time. When those become part of your group's repertoire, then add some more.

6. Creating a Planning Task Force

Who is going to take responsibility for seeing that the retreat actually occurs? Whether one person is designated to do the various tasks or many are designated, WHO is responsible for doing WHAT needs to be established and made clear.

One group divided the responsibility like this:

Three-Person Coordinating Team Plus:

1	music coordinator
4	publicity people
1	artist
1	transportation coordinator
3	registrars
1	nursery coordinator
1	snacks coordinator
18	program group leaders
6	resident leaders

Over thirty were involved in planning!

The tasks of retreat planning CLUSTER in job-relatedness:

Keep this clustering in mind when dividing up responsibilities. Those who are assigned responsibility for one task should work closely with others in their task cluster. Information sharing and coordination are crucial.

The more people involved in planning the more difficult the task of coordination, of "fitting together" all the pieces. Nevertheless, large numbers involved in planning not only distribute the load of work, but also enhance group ownership of the retreat.

If the planning is to be done by committees, then each committee needs a chairperson and a list of "TO DO's." The next fifteen chapters in this manual focus on what TO DO in each of the planning tasks.

The following are principles for the good operation of any task force:

1. The task must be related to group objectives, relevant to needs and priorities.
2. The task is clearly understood.
3. The task is done in a time-line.
4. The task force has the number of people needed to accomplish the task effectively.
5. The task force has *able* personnel.
6. The task is evaluated periodically.
7. The task force is disbanded at the completion of the responsibility.

Using the above principles, the retreat planning task force can be one of ACTION.

7. Goal Setting

A group may well need to grow as a group before it is ready to goal-set explicitly. A retreat can be a tool to help a group gel enough even to begin setting goals.

Goal setting is not easy and not very tangible. Many groups will try to bypass the question of goals and immediately start talking about what they want to DO on the retreat. Goals are implicit in whatever is done, but activity is most helpful when goals can be made explicit. Then the goals can become the agreed-upon common standard by which choices are made and evaluated.

Neglecting the question "Why?" can lead to frustration and dissatisfaction. For example, some retreat participants may refuse to cooperate with the program if their spoken or unspoken goals are different from those which determined the program. (See Retreat Disaster, chapter 3.) Or if goals and purposes are not made clear, some persons may inadvertently create tensions by spreading misinformation.

HOW TO GET STARTED AT GOAL SETTING

One way to begin the planning/goal-setting process is to look at the group "givens" (see Appendix 1 and pp. 17-18):

1. What are the strengths/weaknesses of the group?
2. What are the problems the group faces?
3. What are the needs of the group and individuals in the group?
   a. Why do you come to this group?
   b. What do you want out of it?
4. What are you willing to put into the group as an individual?

Another way to start is to ask group members:

1. What does this group DO? (List.)
2. What is this group FOR? (a different question! List.)

If you are planning a retreat for people from different backgrounds and areas, then you have to make assumptions about them. You also need to be aware of what assumptions you are making. If you assume that the people have certain interests and they don't, you may be in trouble. (All this is not as great a problem if a specific goal/purpose is advertised by the planning group, and participants sign up with accurate knowledge about the event.)

One way to check out assumptions in advance is to have each participant fill out a personal inventory before he or she arrives. (For an example of such a form for youth, see Appendix 10.) This form could be adapted for different groups with other goal-oriented questions included, such as:

1. At the end of this event, I would like to be able to . . .
2. I come to this expecting. . . .
3. I come wanting to experience . . . (or learn).

The replies can be checked against the projected/planned goals of the leadership group, and adjustments can be made if possible. Or the goals can be explained: "We cannot meet all of your expectations; here are the ones we will cover."

In considering the goals for a given retreat, it is important to look at the umbrella goals and purposes for the group. One way to approach this area is to ask:

1. What kinds of people/individuals should we as a group (church) be sending out into the world to minister in Christ's name? What do they look like? How do they act? What are their characteristics, their skills?
2. What kind of group relationships and experiences will make possible that kind of individual?
3. What kind of group leaders will make possible that kind of group?
4. What kinds of experiences and relationships must happen in the lives of the leadership team to make possible that kind of group to make possible that kind of individual?[1]

An *example* of an *umbrella goal* is the goal of Christian education as it has been defined by one denomination:

That all persons be aware of God through his self-disclosure, especially his redeeming love as revealed in Jesus Christ, and, enabled by the Holy Spirit, respond in faith and love; that as new persons in Christ they may know who they are and what their human situation means, grow as sons of God rooted in the Christian community, live in

[1] Adapted from Lloyd Ogilvie, in *Faith/at/Work,* Waco, Texas (August, 1973), p. 11.

obedience to the will of God in every relationship, fulfill their common vocation in the world, and abide in the Christian hope.[2]

The overarching goals of the group can be the starting point for generating specific goals for a retreat. The retreat then becomes a means/vehicle for moving the group along in its purpose. The retreat goals if formulated first may also provide the basis for forming overarching goals.

FORMULATING GOALS

After listing group givens and needs, before actually formulating specific goals statements, it is important that the ideas/concerns/needs generated be categorized and RANKED by relative importance. Those which get the highest ranking can become the focus of the retreat goal statements.

Trying to accomplish too many goals on one retreat will be frustrating when all of them cannot be fulfilled. The purposes of the group, who the people are in the group, and the available time and resources will help determine the kind and realistic number of goals to set and the order in which the goals are to be met.

We have listed a number of goals stated by various individuals for their groups and retreats. (Many could also be umbrella purposes/goals as well as specific retreat goals.) Read through them to see if any are related to your group's goals, or if any might provide starters for a retreat for your group. (See Appendix 3.) Work/discussion sheets are included which can be useful in initiating purpose/goal discussion and identification (Appendixes 4, 5, and 6).

After you have written your potential retreat goal(s) and ranked which are most important, you will want to ask: could the goal be stated more concisely? Are we trying to combine too many things at once? (For example, one group defined its goals as: "Experiencing: 'up-in-out: God, self, others.'" This is a broad, inclusive goal statement. Specific retreat events would focus on one aspect for greater emphasis and focus.)

In planning to reach your goal, it is important to look at the KIND of goal you have stated or selected. Is it informational or conceptual? Is it attitudinal? Is it experiential? Or is it a combination of these?

Specific goals can be categorized by looking at the desired changes we hope to see happen. They can be:

knowing: (informational/conceptual/cognitive goals) for example, "to *know* who we are. . . ."

feeling: (attitudinal goals/changes in values or feelings) for example, "to be *aware* of God . . ."; "to *abide* in the Christian hope. . . ."

experiential: (doing/being the new person desired) for example, "to *respond* in faith . . ."; "to *become* . . .; to *grow* . . .; to *live* . . .; to *fulfill*. . . ."[3]

(For further explanation and practice in categorizing goal statements, see Appendix 7.)

Being aware of the KIND OF GOALS is important in determining the MEANS which will best achieve the goal. The MEANS to a given goal needs to be consistent with the goal if it is to be effectively reached.

The program resources and scheduling chapters will be helpful in pointing you to related materials for developing and choosing ways to achieve your stated goal. The goal is your HANDLE for:

- selecting from among the many options where to go and what to do on the retreat.
- deciding how closely to stick to the plans during the retreat.
- evaluating whether the retreat has accomplished what the group expected and wanted it to.

---

[2] *Foundations for Curriculum* (Valley Forge: American Baptist Board of Education and Publication, 1966), p. 13.

[3] Martha M. Leypoldt, *Learning Is Change* (Valley Forge: Judson Press, 1971). pp. 34-35.

8. Program

Programming and scheduling are planning activities that are hard for some to separate. Our distinction is that the schedule is the FORM; the program is the CONTENT. In programming, you decide what ideas and activity elements are to be included in the retreat; in scheduling, you proportion the amount of time to be given to each and arrange the order and place. Programming and scheduling need to be compatible.

With a clear understanding of the goals to be accomplished and a knowledge of WHO is going, decision making about the program can begin.

INTRODUCTION TO PROGRAMMING

IN ONE SENSE, PROGRAM IS EVERYTHING THAT HAPPENS ON THE RETREAT. The most "teachable moments" may occur at times other than the planned focused educational, inspirational, or discussion times. The talked-about program can be reinforced or contradicted by the lived program of everything else that occurs: for example, sleeping arrangements, handling of meals, and methods of problem solving. All activities can become resources to the program.

One cannot plan everything that happens on the retreat (thank goodness!). Some of the program ELEMENTS that CAN be thought about beforehand and chosen to develop for content include:

presentations	sleep arrangements
experiential education	eating/fasting
discussion/dialogue	decision making
prayer	planning
worship	evaluating
expressive arts	maintenance
silence	service
play	witnessing

These program elements are familiar as activities of our daily and church life. However, the time-out and apartness of the retreat setting provide opportunity for experimenting with doing these activities in different ways and in greater depth.

Variety in programming can be created by:

1. selecting some elements for emphasis

2. varying the amount of time
   - structure
   - people
   - choice
   - noise
   - focus
   - energy level

Awareness of these factors which influence program experience can help us shape programs more congruent with our goals. Many retreat planners have fallen in love with a certain type of program and schedule which has worked well in the past. Beware! If the people and goals for the retreat are different this year, last year's program (no matter how carefully followed) will *not* fill the bill. (See Retreat Disaster in chapter 3.)

Some generalizations can be made about what type of program element enhances which goals. If the major goal is one of the following—building relationships, having fun, providing service, or broadening experience—then larger proportions of time, noise, and energy level should be planned for experiential DOING program elements. If the major goal is to increase intellectual awareness of Christian concepts, one could expect that the amount of PRESENTATIONAL time would be greater with more structure and less noise. The goals of personal evangelism and personal growth can be well implemented by either the presentational or the experiential style.

Outside resource people are particularly effective in retreats aimed at expanding concepts and also for those focused on evangelism and personal growth. An outside resource person (unless functioning as facilitator) could work as a detriment to retreats aimed at team-building, leadership development, service or fun, by claiming time for listening instead of for doing.

We are mentioning these commonsense generalizations because we have witnessed retreats which have violated this program-goal harmony. At one extreme: in the name of increasing the experience of Christian love among participants, a highly structured presentational program was planned with little time for small group or people interaction. It missed the boat. At the other extreme: in the name of increasing personal spiritual growth, there was little intense input planned, with people left up to their own resources. They became bored and restless, and a real opportunity to encourage change was missed. These mistakes can happen when we select the program first and then attach a fine sounding goal or when our talked-about goal does not match our gut-goal.

Program Alternatives. Have a number of "Plan B's" in your hat for a rainy day, for people looking for something to do during free time, or for replacement of a program idea which no longer seems relevant. Short movies and craft materials can be developed into program options if needed. Have some extra materials along as resources for planning worship. Some recreation ideas can be created on the spot using the resources of the retreat location: a midnight hike or a short excursion into town. Ask the facility director about the resources in the area.

An Extra. If you reproduce a written program for participants (helpful when the program is complex, long, or with many options), remember to package it attractively. There are inexpensive ways. Colored paper, unusual folding, or creative drawing and layout can add a lot. Clarity of information should not be sacrificed, however, to design.

The remainder of this chapter is organized according to the major goals which the program intends to implement. We have broadly classified retreat goals as focusing on one of the following areas of Christian life-style:

1. Building the Body of Christ

   a. Developing a group; family   Relational
   b. Planning for future group life
   c. Developing leadership   Feeling

2. Personal growth

3. Conceptual growth   Knowing

4. Experiencing the world

5. Service   Doing[1]

6. Evangelism

There is some overlapping in this as in any classification system. All retreats assume "spiritual growth" as a goal. The category of "personal growth" includes those programs aimed at the person as a spiritual individual with a need to focus on one aspect or to integrate many of the multiple life functions. These categories are offered as handles to help you find program ideas and resources to implement your group's goal. (For additional program ideas organized by program goal and by activity—openers, closers, worship, Bible study, group builders—see Program Ideas Chart.)

[1] Martha M. Leypoldt, *Learning Is Change* (Valley Forge: Judson Press, 1971), p. 44.

BUILDING THE BODY OF CHRIST

Developing Group Life as Christians

The retreats in this section are aimed primarily at building the accepting, loving community which fosters human growth. The focus is on getting to know people in the group more deeply; developing trust and communication skills; celebrating togetherness, commonesses, and differences; and learning skills to resolve interpersonal tensions in the group.

THE WIZARD OF ID   by Brant parker and Johnny hart

By permission of John Hart and Field Enterprises, Inc.

All of the sample programs which we have received in this category are planned for YOUTH, with the exception of those for the specific groups of families and marriage partners. This may indicate that for youth the church group may be the locus of the youths' primary social relationships while for adults the primary social relationship is not any church group in which they participate but rather their chosen marriage and family. Or perhaps adults do not know yet what they are missing in not extending the "at-homeness" that develops from this kind of retreat beyond their biological family to include others.

There is a great deal of variety in the extent of structure of retreats planned for *junior highs*. Some retreats promise joy and celebration at just being together and doing fun things. In the retreat planned by Scottsville Baptist Church there is more structure utilizing group-process techniques and some traditional forms for spiritual and relational growth—alone time and foot-washing. (See Appendix 23.) Appendix 25 offers interaction and small-group opportunities and demands a high degree of participation on the part of all. The worship service drew upon the expressive activities of the small group and included ceremonies of Communion and renewal of commitment. For an example of a more complexly planned retreat, see Appendix 24. This retreat was highly experiential, offering unique group-building exercises with frequent changes of pace and varied resources.

The same variety is evident in retreats planned for *youth of all ages.*

PROS:

1. Good opportunity to develop relationships between different age groups other than own in family.

2. Chance to break through the "wall" set up by many school systems. Retreat living exposure helps with the discovering that people are not so different.

3. Represents part of the "real world" where many ages of people work together based on interest and skill rather than age.

WHY HAVE AN ALL-YOUTH RETREAT?

CONS:

1. Older youth sometimes resist having younger kids along. (Can be overcome if can change the attitude from competition for status to the attitude that each age has unique things to give.)

2. Due to different maturities and interests, one has to plan for more options in the retreat program.

3. Need more leaders to implement.

We recommend retreats for all youth on occasion, not to replace retreats by age groups but rather to supplement them. Examples follow.

The First Baptist Church of Los Angeles, under the leadership of the associate pastor Arlo Reichter, has planned several fun trips for all youth with no formal program. A unique feature was their staying in motels. Benefits emerged as Christians and new recruits lived and did things together. Another all-youth retreat sponsored by this church provided a great deal more structure, including small-group time focused on developing trust, honesty, and celebration. An evaluation element was included. An outstanding feature of this retreat was the small-group leaders' instruction sheet—it was a clear,

humorous, and helpful guide with goals and how-to suggestions. The Hatboro Baptist Church in Pennsylvania sponsored a retreat aimed to increase communication and trust across age-group lines and to develop more group strength within the age groups. A unique feature of this retreat was the participational worship service planned ahead of time with creative program folders mimeographed by some of the older youth.

The examples of *senior high* retreats show by and large more intensity of focus. The First Baptist Church of Kansas City, Missouri, had a theme of "Reaching for the Stars" and utilized an outside resource person skilled in leading "Serendipity" group experiences. In addition, the group allowed retreat time to plan for the church's Youth Sunday. From the First Presbyterian Church in Oceanside, California, comes a snow-camp retreat which incorporated a rieh variety of expressive and experiential activity to foster personal growth and group building. Guidelines for cinquain, Bible passage translations, and group games—Prisoners' Dilemma, Love Gifts, and Intimacy Game—were included. A good example of program preparation and follow-through comes from Rev. Revis Turner, First Baptist Church in Lima, Ohio, whose senior high group used a retreat for intensifying koinonia. The late rap session, after pizza the first evening, and other times scheduled for singing, Bible study, conversational prayer, and spontaneous sharing were apparently quite meaningful. The state youth officers who came as guests functioned as leaven in the midst, giving their personal testimony—a very effective use of outside resource people congruent with the group's goal.

It becomes evident that few of these retreat programs had much in the way of presentation. Several used filmstrips or movies as input. Several used witnessing and Bible study. Most used as material the living persons of the retreat participants in expressive activities.

Developing a Marriage or Family Group

The Roman Catholic Church has pioneered in weekend retreating for married couples in the "Marriage Encounter," seeking to enrich already good marriages. These weekends feature lay leadership (Marriage Encounter alumni) and usually a priest. They are highly structured, moving from testimonial presentation on a subject to alone time and to dialogue time with the marriage partner. The fellowshipping with other couples comes during reunions. Subjects covered include: "How I See Myself"; "My Contribution"; problem areas, such as sex, children, time, relatives, money, death; and spiritual growth.

Lynn Nelson

Similar in intensity of focus and in goals is a "Marriage Enrichment Retreat" held by the First Baptist Church in San Bruno, California. The specific purpose was to improve communication and intimacy in the marriage relationship. The couples received input from the Bible, tapes, various measuring instruments, an article, and verbal and nonverbal experiential exercises.

The Pastoral Counseling and Communication Center in San Carlos, California, offers a highly structured face-to-face couple interaction in their Marriage Renewal Retreat.

We have experienced a three-day couples' retreat sponsored by the Philadelphia Lutheran Churches which not only focused on married couple interaction but also structured many other chances for practicing interaction, decision making, and communication skills. Feedback from others observing us as a couple and the opportunity to witness other examples of marriage were significant added dimensions for us.

Family Building

"A retreat on family communication can come to your church." So advertises the Pastoral Counseling and Communication Center of the First Baptist Church of San Carlos, California. Large- and small-group sessions making use of the tool of role play are featured to explore these topics:
1. The First Rule in Meaningful Interpersonal Relationships
2. Husband-Wife Communication
3. The Use of Responsibility with Youth
4. How to Relate to the Guilty
5. The Art of Setting Limits, with Sibling Rivals, with the Rebellious, with Martyrs

Increasing communication between parents and children is one primary goal of the Parent Effectiveness Training program. People all over the country have received special training to lead the 8-session Parent Effectiveness Training series. Dr. Thomas Gordon, the founder, has also written a book called *Parent Effectiveness Training*[2] which can be used for discussion or role play in retreat planning and programming.

Family Cluster education and training experiences are emerging across the country. Also, some churches are experimenting in the establishment of community residences made up of a group of nuclear families. (Acts 2:43-47 describes what seems to be a similar movement in the early church.)

The whole area of family retreating is one just beginning to be explored. Many churches are doing it, but few seem to have developed a special program to maximize on family members being together. For example, some churches are combining family camping with planning retreats but with little cross-generational programming except for recreation, meals, and sleeping. In one retreat, Sunday school was age-graded, missing the opportunity for family experiences in study and worship.

Value does come from sharing with other family groups informally. However, not many retreats seem to have the major goal of strengthening families. Here is a frontier!

Planning for the Future of the Group

Quite a few churches have annual planning retreats. Often these are one-day affairs including time for recreation, fellowshipping around a meal, and worship. Sometimes, little time is devoted to specific planning.

The Annual Planning Conferences of the First Baptist Church of San Bruno, California, are an exception. These retreats have allowed for an evening, overnight, and a full day. They feature warm-up communication exercises to

[2] Thomas Gordon, *Parent Effectiveness Training* (New York: Peter H. Wyden, 1970).

prepare for the planning tasks. Each yearly retreat does not expect to cover all the planning elements, but each year's task is to build on the previous. For example, in 1969, the focus was on the mission of the church and parish renewal. The 1971 retreat focused on long-range goal setting and budget ideas. The 1972 focus was on the purpose of the church and the planning process. See Appendix 43 for a sample schedule and list of questions for committee planning.

Another church which takes yearly planning seriously is the National Baptist Memorial Church of Washington, D.C. Careful thought and much resource are given to develop their planning weekend Program Manual. Their booklet includes schedule, songs, graces, table prayers, list of planners, short inspirational quotations, and even a cartoon on teamwork. At one planning weekend, for *three days* people of all age groups met for planning, recreation, and spiritual growth. Only four formal planning sessions were held in the three days' time. However, the planning sessions were not intended to cover the whole of the church program, but each session was used for people to meet in groups for specific areas of church program to evaluate, brainstorm, and commit themselves to new action. There were eighteen different planning groups meeting four times and then reporting back to the group as a whole. Many specifics in planning were accomplished.

Perhaps less cumbersome would be for different boards and groups in the church to have their own planning retreats. *Youth* groups have used retreats for this purpose. Westminster Presbyterian Church of Springfield, Illinois, has used an experiential approach to encourage youth in developing planning ability. Specific plans were made for their group. One retreat was used to start an expressive project to provide input for many group meetings to come. (See Appendix 26.)

Choir groups have often held practice retreats, preparing for future presentations.

The Board of Christian Education of Hatboro Baptist Church in Pennsylvania had a successful planning retreat utilizing an assignment sheet for fact gathering and reflection on issues to be filled out PRIOR to the retreat and used as a working sheet. (See Appendix 45.)

A successful area-wide Christian Education Committee planning retreat was held by the Philadelphia Baptist Association in less than a 24-hour period. Friday evening the group met for team-building exercises, evaluation of the past year's work, and agenda input. On Saturday morning after breakfast and wake-ups, the group decided on team priorities for the next year and had a resource sharing time. After lunch break with more wake-ups, the group developed specific objectives for an area-wide training event for church leaders, and assignments of tasks were made. The retreat closed with worship in song and word.

The Reverend Milton Owens has found his "Leadership Workbook for Christian Education in Black Churches" helpful for several Board of Education's planning sessions. (See Appendix 46.) (For some planning tools, see Appendixes 6, 8, 9, and 42.)

Church groups and boards can use a planning retreat to:

1. Discuss and define and gain consensus on philosophy, goals; the functions of the group and its members. TUNE-IN to God's will.
2. Rank priorities for future involvement.
3. Clarify divisions of labor, develop or improve job descriptions.
4. Develop specific program units.
5. Define and propose resolutions to problems.
6. Build TEAM SPIRIT: mutual support and appreciation of each person's talents, limitations, and contributions.

Remember! Retreats can be used to plan retreats.

Developing Leadership

A challenging memo from the pastor was sent to all board members of the Greenville Baptist Church in Greenville, Rhode Island, inviting them to a leadership retreat. The retreat was short (appealing to adult time schedules) but included one overnight and was chock-full, fitting in five task sessions on leadership development, two Bible study sessions, a "what the church is" collage, and a celebration, plus some free time for getting-acquainted activity. The task sessions included reviewing characteristics of a Christian leader, team building, and goal setting. (See Appendix 47.) The Board of Education felt that the retreat was so important that they made the retreat available free. Thirty of the seventy-three board members attended the 1972 retreat. Church leaders came back strengthened and inspired. It has become an annual happening.

A film retreat, sponsored by the Diocese of Richmond, Virginia, Department of Religious Education and Liturgy, was used to train religious educators of youth in Virginia at two locations and on two dates. An exciting format with emphasis on Christian community in large- and small-group sessions was used to encourage Christian educators in motivation and ability to use relevant films for developing the spiritual life of their youth. For information about training opportunities, see the List of Resources in Section IV of this book.

PROGRAMS FOR PERSONAL GROWTH

When the primary purpose of the retreat is to deepen the individual's experience of himself or herself as a child of God, then one program element seems indispensable: planned time for individual devotion—reading, reflection, meditation, prayer, and listening. This alone time may be more or less structured depending on the newness of the participants' experience with creative use of such time. Beginners need more structure than those older in the faith. However, at times new input and structure is helpful for freshening or moving out of a rut the devotional practice of the faithful. (See Appendix 48, "A Workshop on Prayer," for a retreat which was structured to teach people how better to use alone time.)

The programs we have seen vary in the proportion of *alone time* to group time. The program day at Kirkridge Retreat Center for Protestants in Bangor, Pennsylvania, offers a great deal of silent time even while people are in group activity, extending the amount of personal time. The Retreat Center emphasizes the importance of experiencing "quiet" which can so easily be dispelled even by fervent devotion. Many other retreat planners have scheduled time at the rising or closing of each day for silent devotions. It is possible to have an evening, a morning, or a full day of silence.

Some retreats have been structured so that the bulk of time is spent as a group but the focus of those in the group is upon self in relationship to God. It is as though many individuals are gathered to be guided into spending profitable time with themselves and their Lord. This seems to be the purpose of a retreat on "Celebration" planned for senior highers using multimedia resources to create a personal trip celebrating events, birth, death, life, and NOW. (See Appendix 28.) Two other quite effective examples of this structure are a women's retreat, "A Day Apart" (see Appendix 52), and a Deacons' Retreat (see Appendix 53). Both are quite intense days of discipline, highly structured. The Deacons' Retreat offers unique features of optional fasting and the giving up of wrist watches. In the women's retreat it was found that too much had been planned and time ran short. Both utilized a booklet containing instructions and space for personal reply. Other group experiences which might be a part of such retreats of discipline are a vigil and physical-meditative exercises.

Programs for personal growth vary also in the amount of opportunity for individuals to express their commitment. At the "Heavy Happening" in Ohio, singing and conversational prayer led to testimonies, confessions, repentance, and rejoicing. A retreat using multimedia for expression of faith was the "Choose Life Retreat," an ecumenical event at First Presbyterian Church in Parkersburg, West Virginia. Participants attended two workshops out of nine choices: drama, art, the film, church and radio, experimental worship, folk hymns, poetry–dance, "Top-Ten Theology" (pop music), and "What's New in Youth Work?" The closing worship service was planned from the various elements created in the workshops. A beautiful format for personal testimony is the "Candlelight Forum" used at the Unitarian Church of Arlington, Virginia, family retreat. In an atmosphere of candlelight, four people share "What I Believe and Why." Another way of encouraging personal commitment is the use of a written "Commitment Statement," perhaps to be renewed yearly. The Quaker form of worship with no formal leader but with opportunity for each to bring forth a thought, prayer, song, or question can encourage individual expression of faith. (People not used to this form of worship may need and want preparation time in advance.) Another possibility is the use of symbolic *acts* of commitment, such as the joining of hands, burning of paper idols, foot washing, or communion.

The amount of *structured time* on the retreat geared for personal growth seems to vary from one extreme to the other, the least effective being in the middle range. The Kirkridge, Deacons', and Women's retreats all call for individual conformity to a chosen discipline—highly structured. In contrast, the Capon Springs, Virginia, Unitarian Retreat (see Appendix 49) provides activity options for many time slots, taking into account not only the wide age span among participants but also the need for participants to find their own rhythm and pace for spiritual renewal.

Personal growth programs differ in their proportion of *head-learning* time versus *experiential-learning* time. Most of the retreats mentioned above have a heavy emphasis on DOING—experiential learning. The retreat programs which are presentational in nature, utilizing speakers, movies, and readings to develop Christian identity, allow for some discussion time or silence as a way to integrate the presentation material into one's personal life. For a superb example of a balance of presentation and integration time, see Appendix 29. In this retreat sponsored by the Vine Street Christian Church in Nashville, Tennessee, contemporary music pretaped plus the Bible were the major inputs for serious study and self-searching for senior highs studying Jesus. Badges with the theme title gave youth a fun chance to express their commitment.

Because people are complex and have so many possible involvements, the variety in *themes* of personal-growth programs is immense. Here are some of the areas of possible focus for discovering and applying Christianity to persons:

Who Am I? (See Program Ideas Chart for ideas.)
Personality
Life-Style/Everyday Life
Our Bodies (dress, food, drugs, sex, rest, exercise)
Loneliness
Being a Student
Selecting and Developing a Career (See Program Ideas Chart.)
Christian on the Job
Parenting
Being a Church Member (Appendix 42)
Being a Servant
Being a Follower of Christ
Handling Problems
Daring to Trust
Are We Free?
Valuing (See Program Ideas Chart.)

Talents and Gifts
Being a Man
Being a Woman
Being a Leader
Being a Teenager
Being Old
Going to College
In the Military
Being an Athlete
Being an Engineer
Being a Voter
Being a Citizen
Being an Individual
Being Married
Being a Friend
Owning Things
Owning Feelings

From this listing, one could feel that all retreats belong in this personal growth category. The programs in this section are those which challenge the person to integrate Christianity into his or her life as an *individual.* (Those which focus on the person as a relating being are included in BUILDING THE BODY OF CHRIST.) Personal-growth retreats serve to enhance the individual's feeling of "at-homeness" in the universe, anchorage in Christ.

Whether a program fulfills the purpose of personal growth or that of increasing knowledge of Christianity depends on the amount of time allowed in programming for digestion of the input and participation in the output. If there is very little program time for such synthesizing activity and the emphasis is upon feeding in new information and ways of thinking about life, then we classify the program as CONCEPTUAL GROWTH. Bible study can be done with either emphasis.

CONCEPTUAL GROWTH

Many exciting retreat programs have been created to stimulate the mind and extend the grasp of understanding of the Christian faith.

A variety of media can be used: speakers, panels, slides, movies, tapes of music, readings, TV or radio shows, records, books, plays, posters, murals, and others.

The range of stimuli can be from the study of one passage in the Bible to a retreat with twenty-six films. The amount of required individual advance preparation for programs can vary greatly from bringing oneself to bringing a favorite thing or to reading an entire book.

All ages can be interested in intellectual growth. For an excellent outline of a retreat to encourage theological thinking among eighth graders, see "Retreat Stimulates Eighth-Grade Theologians" by Tracy Early in the *Baptist Leader,* January, 1972, pages 50-53. In this weekend retreat held by Riverside Church in New York City, they found that junior highers were willing to spend eight to ten hours of solid study when personally involved in considering the ideas and when a fair amount of scheduled recreation time was allowed. The group was divided into four caucus groups to develop statements of beliefs about God, Jesus, man, sin, forgiveness, and the church. Input was given by slides, questions, the Apostles' Creed, and examples of statements of faith. The young people responded with words, skits, and their own statements. The four groups then negotiated together for one statement about each area of belief in their "Beliefs Council." The final statements were included in the closing worship. Three times of study on Saturday were broken by meals, three hours of outdoor recreation after lunch, refreshments, and a late evening "Delegates" party. (Singing can also provide a good transition from play to study.)

A retreat exploring "Change" for All-Youth was

sponsored by the Grinnell, Iowa, United Methodist Youth Council. It was particularly rich in the use of resources—films, books, the Bible, cartoons, tapes of TV programs, a NASA simulation game, crafts, and a retreat booklet adapted from the unit on "Change" in Argus Communication's "Choose Life" program. The format was youth-led small groups using the resource booklet as a guide. This structure not only allowed for thought stimulation but also for leadership development and deepening bonds between group members. (See Appendix 30.)

A retreat for adults on the same subject of "Change" was done through testimony, speaker, discussion and panel sharing. (See Appendix 50.)

For summaries of a retreat rich in variety of theme resources, see "Our Country: Right or Wrong?" (Appendix 31).

Several film retreats have been exciting and successful. The First Baptist Church in Madison, Wisconsin (Rev. W. Lee Hicks), sponsored one which was centered upon exploring three themes from *West Side Story*. All in the group had seen the play or movie. With the novel as the textbook and with records for the music, the group explored "The Gospel Confronts Teen Culture" looking at the themes "You ain't never been my age," "A Jet all the way" (gang culture), and "When love comes so strong" (the bridging power of love). Another retreat utilized nine films to explore with high schoolers four major themes: war, violence, poverty, and sex. (See Appendix 32.)

Specially prepared retreat booklets can bring together excerpts from many sources for mind stretching. Some have been quite creative in layout. (See Appendix 33.)

The possible program *themes* for the learning retreat are as varied and numerous as the earth and the heavens. Themes may range from personal freedom, nature, history, politics, economics, and art, to theology. Lists of subjects for possible study as Christians have been brainstormed by youth. (See Appendix 11.) Hold a brainstorming session with your group to come up with new theme ideas.

Note: Included in the Appendix is a description of resources and methods to explore the theme of death and life. Although these ideas were not carried out in a retreat setting, many are unique and would add richly to a retreat program on this theme. (See Appendix 51.)

For further sources to develop theme ideas, see the Program Ideas Chart.

EXPERIENCING THE WORLD

Retreats aimed at broadening the experiential base of the participants can range from simple to complex, long-

Lynn Nelson

distance to short hauls, quick ones to long term. ALL hold ADVENTURE!

Travel Retreats

Short, simple and fun retreats for city youth to experience new locations, fresh air, and nature were held by the First Baptist Church of Los Angeles. The group traveled to area entertainment attractions, such as "Sea World," and stayed at group rates in motels. Hatboro Baptist post-high group (Pennsylvania) sponsored an overnight canoeing-camping trip for inner-city and suburban poverty youngsters. Nine high school youth from three churches in Philadelphia and the suburbs went to

New York City to witness and study city poverty and international relations. (See the evaluation sheet for details and focus—Appendix 20.)

A fun inexpensive way to broaden the experiences of a group is to plan *youth-exchanges* between churches in different areas: geographical, racial, economic, cultural, or denominational. See Appendix 34 for a specific case example. Youth exchange can also be a way to build a larger group to plan for longer trips.

Longer trips. These vary in destination, mode of transportation, structure, and expense. Some take close to a year of planning. Five examples follow: (See the chart at the end of this section of the chapter for comparison of the five trips described here.)

1. After two short practice rides, a seven-day *bike trip* was begun by youth from the Grinnell United Methodist Church (Iowa) as a bike mission for Key '73. Letters were sent to Methodist churches along the route ahead of time to arrange for accommodations, meals, and sharing with other youth groups. One car drove ahead of the bicyclists to set up break and refreshment stops. This group, like others planning longer trips, had some difficulty in recruiting adult leaders who could be available for the whole week.

2. Three Baptist churches in the East planned one-week *recreational* experience trips to places like Canada, Kentucky, and the Jersey shore. The trips were preceded by youth exchanges between the churches. One year eighty youth participated. Program included visiting special attractions and vespers with singing, discussion, and devotions around the campfire.

3. A low-cost one-week *study tour* of poverty in rural West Virginia was undertaken by the First Baptist Church of Ridley Park, Pennsylvania, under the leadership of Larry Dobson. Unique features included the program resources of Alderson-Broaddus College's sociology department and two nights' free lodging; interviewing city and county employees and community organizers; visiting poverty areas, churches, a backwoods music festival, an old folks' home; AND four days of living in a primitive cabin—wood stove, hand water pump, outhouse, and no electricity. (The group did not visit merely as observers. They sang and participated in the life of the institutions/churches they visited.) Slides and tapes made during the tour were used by the youth to create a sound-film presentation and program which was shared with over forty churches after the two groups returned home.

4. Dallas Lutheran Youth, led by John Junke and Glenn Oswald, have sponsored two "*Get Out Of Texas*" (GOOT I and II) trips primarily for high school juniors and seniors. The first GOOT spent two weeks in the Denver-Rockies area. GOOT II was two weeks of travel in rented VW vans which included visits to Chicago, St. Louis, and six days in the Ozark mountains for nature, recreation, and folk-culture experiences. (See Appendix 35 for details.)

5. A three-week cross-country trip including a week's sailing in the Bahamas was sponsored by Trinity Lutheran Church, Ventura, California, and was led by Joel Bjerkestrand. Vehicles used were a 27-foot motor home lent to the group by the S.C. Lutheran Camping Association, and a 65-foot sailing ship. The travel fellowship was heightened by forming three groups of five youth with rotating responsibility for meals, cleanup, and Bible study (Ephesians) presentation each day. Creativity and participation were high.

The ship and program crew were provided by CRUISE, *C*hristian *R*enewal *U*nderway *I*n the *S*ailing *E*xperience. On shipboard, evening sharing included a group process called "circling." (See Appendix 36.)

Hometown Adventure

Traveling and visiting are not the only means of enlarging experience. Christians who are called to be the "salt of the earth" can find right within their own city or town people and places which are usually "out of bounds"—people in different age categories, in hospitals or other institutions, in different political, vocational, economic, social, religious, or geographic groupings.

A task force of youth from Philadelphia, with the help of Larry Waltz of the Philadelphia Baptist Association and the Pennsylvania/Delaware Baptists, planned a Friday and Saturday *Youth Cultural Exchange.* A total of forty black Americans, Puerto Ricans, Burmese, Thai, Chinese, Japanese, Africans, Italians, Haitians, Hawaiians, and Caucasians gathered to share the foods, recreation, artifacts, art, music, dance, clothing, and folk traditions of their cultural heritage.

Task groups handled the planning for meals, devotions, music, recreation, and presentations-sharing. The exchange provided ample opportunity for study, comparison, understanding, and appreciation for each other's cultures and strengthened Christian commitment and fellowship.

Trip Comparisons

Time	Goal—Experience	Vehicle & Destination	Program Uniqueness	Total Number	Leader—Participant Ratio	Cost	Who Sponsored
1 Week	Key '73—Mission Unity	Bicycles; 140 miles in Iowa	Stayed in churches; Shared with other youth groups	10	1:4		Betsy Bouska, C.E. Dir., United Methodist Church, Grinnell, Iowa
1 Week Trips	Recreation Fellowship	Cars; at different times: Canada, Kentucky, N.J. shore	Outdoor sports & recreation—e.g., caving, sight-seeing	Range 30 to 80	1:6	$25—$30 per person	The Reverends Larry Dobson, Bob Salmons, Jack Minear, Baptists in the East
1 Week	Study of Poverty	Cars; Barbour Co., West Virginia	Soc. Dept., Alderson-Broaddus College gov't. officials, community organizations, churches, homes, music fest, primitive cabin slides & taping	8	1:7	$20 per person	Rev. Larry Dobson (First Baptist Church Ridley Park, Pa.) now at First Baptist Church, Trenton, N.J.
2 Weeks	Understand various forms of ministry; Recreation; Folk Culture	Rented VW vans, Chicago, St. Louis, Ozarks	Walther League Brd. for Youth Min., Concordia Seminary, Luth. School of Nursing, Concordia Teacher's College, Valparaiso Univ., camping, canoeing, folk-art exhibits	40	1:7	$75 per person	The Reverends Glenn Oswald, John Junke, Dallas Lutheran Youth, Dallas, Texas
3 Weeks Plus	See Country & Ocean; grow as a "family"	27' Motor home 65' Sailing ship California to Bahamas	sailing, snorkling, creative Bible study, stayed at churches, "Circling" group process, movies of trip	17	1:7 for 2 weeks 1:2 for week on ship	$250 per person (includes $160 for cruise)	Rev. Joel Bjerkestrand Trinity Lutheran Church, Ventura, Calif. with Conrad Bratten c/o CRUISE, Box 755 Miami, FL 33143

With a little imagination and some planning, whole new worlds can be experienced right *in your own church* facility or nearby retreat location. The bulk of time on a retreat can be focused on one living situation for the group to experience. Each person lives an assigned role until the end, when each sheds the role and debriefs, sharing feelings and evaluation. Examples of such focused role-play activity include:

1. a blind day
2. a day of complete silence
3. a poverty weekend
4. a racial-encounter weekend
5. an ecology weekend
6. biblical simulations

These "pretend" situations, if agreed to by all ahead of time and followed through consistently, can be very powerful and real. They offer new experiences of the life-death forces within each of us and in the world. They are potentially stimulating for emotional, conceptual, and spiritual growth. Because they are powerful—awakening deep emotions—a plenteous number of mature folks may be needed for conflict resolution and counseling. Junior highs can usually tolerate only a short game. Longer time periods require more attention and deeper levels of commitment to the experiment and therefore are more appropriate for older teens and adults.

Program *elements* which can heighten the experiential type of retreat are:

1. movies which bring an immediacy of setting and feeling to the learning about new aspects of the world.
2. participation in the discovery of a new person, place, or thing by an interview, individual time to explore and assimilate, or reading.
3. guides, people who know more about the experience than the explorers.
4. worship services which incorporate the new learnings into worldview.

SERVICE

Many opportunities for service are available. Ways to find the needs include asking the pastor or church boards; using your own eyes to look at the community; reading in newspapers, magazines, and religious publications about service opportunities; and checking with human service agencies and denominational departments of missions.

Retreats can be used to do a major service task in one time period or to initiate a service program which entails a longer-range commitment. Service projects which are do-able in one weekend are usually "fix-up," "clean-up," *thing* oriented. Service to *people* usually requires some continuity and follow-up.

Examples of service projects which are appropriate for retreats are: creating and giving programs for institutionalized people; participating in ecology cleanup; and fixing, building, painting, or cleaning community centers, homes, churches, or denominational facilities.

You may need to arrange for special training sessions to help your group understand the nature of the project, the people involved, and the skills which will be required. (For planning tools, see the List of Resources.)

Service retreats can be quite inexpensive. The facility you are serving may provide free lodging and help with the meals. If the location of your service project is not far from your home church, the group could stay overnight at your church (giving opportunity for the hassles and joys of living together) and travel by day to the project location.

Meaning. Pay attention to the way in which the work assignments are given—some methods can be divisive rather than group building. Provide some other group-building activity during the retreat and some celebration-meditation time for the individual participants to chew on "what for" questions. Service can be rendered at the expense of the receiver if the servant's attitudes are patronizing or full of irritation. Doers of real service are enabled to give to others from their own experience of being loved.

Balance. The Friends in Philadelphia advertise their weekend work camp as a "treasure hunt." They are asking people fifteen years or older to DIG IN to social, racial, and economic problems of the city by becoming involved in an experience which balances hard work with learning exposures, good refreshment, and contrasting worship times. (See Appendix 37.) Many local and regional groups have coordinated service projects through this work camp. There may be a similar setup in a nearby community; if not, perhaps you could start one.

BEING BUSY DOING SERVICE is not in itself great. If the service is concerned, respectful LOVE ACTION—WOW!

EVANGELISM

Sharing the truth may be part of many retreats, but it can also be the primary thrust of the entire retreat time.

Some retreats focus on *preparing* folks for evangelizing. ECUPAX '73 was a gathering of six hundred youth at a hotel in Philadephia, sponsored by the Philadelphia Baptist Association for a one-day preparatory session on personal evangelism. It concluded in a dramatic way with a group proclamation by a candlelight prayer processional through the streets to a cathedral. See Appendix 38 for discussion questions and a worksheet.

For a weekend retreat on preparation for evangelizing, see the detailed description in Appendix 39.

Several ideas for programming the *doing* of evangelism on retreats are:

1. Sharing signs, pass-outs, or singing on a bike trip or walk.
2. Teaching and using the Kennedy Coral-Ridge or the "Winsome" approach during the retreat to share Christ with retreat participants.
3. Applying Bob Dent's ideas for "Electric Christianity" involving 9th and 10th graders in street interviewing and creating TV and radio spots which share Christ. (See Appendix 40.)
4. Planning the retreat near a major resort area and planning ways and time to talk with people informally about their direction in life.

The service-project retreat may be a beautiful opportunity for demonstrating the love of Christ and thus witnessing to those around you.

Retreat programs in each goal category will at their best be workshops for strengthening one's life in Christ, thereby enabling one better to serve and share.

9. Resources

Note: Complete information on all resources mentioned in this chapter will be found in the List of Resources in Section IV.

Resources are everywhere. ANYTHING can be used as a resource for your group! All you need to do is to decide upon your goals and then use your creativity. Resources as such are NEUTRAL in that they are not inherently "spiritual" or "carnal." They "become" spiritual or secular in their application and use.

Use the following questions to help generate resource ideas with your group:

1. What are you doing for fun in your spare time? What are your favorite TV shows? Record albums? Radio stations? Magazines? Books? Movies?

2. What are the special talents among the group members? Music? Crafts? Special knowledge or interests?

3. If working with youth, spend fifteen minutes a day listening to a pop radio station in your area or reading youth-oriented magazines (*Mad, Rolling Stones, Hot Rod, Seventeen,* etc.)

4. Take any common object—paper clips, rubber bands, coke cans, etc.—and brainstorm ways it could be used related to a theme, or ways it is representative of your Christian faith.

There are a number of ways to get resources without paying for them directly. It depends on the kinds of things you need and how far in advance you begin to plan. Permanent items, such as tape recorders or audiovisual equipment, may be donated as Christmas "gifts" to the youth or the board of Christian education. (Of course it helps Santa to make a Christmas WISH LIST and to publish it!) Include a variety of books, materials, games, and their prices.

Media materials abound: comic strips in the newspapers; taped portions of radio, TV programs; edited portions of the evening news; old commercials no longer being used by TV and radio stations; developed film and test strips and unused photoprints from high school or college photo classes; used negatives and acetate from printing/lithograph companies for use in making slides. See the manuals listed in the resource section for other ideas.

Special resource leaders can be obtained by asking your pastor or other pastors in the area who would qualify in a particular field. If your church is near a college/university, professors are often willing to be resource people, or they can refer you to someone else. Denominational offices have contact with many people in a wide area. Write to them; describe the kind of person you are looking for; and get suggestions.

Ministers are often willing to "trade-off." "I will come and be an 'expert' for your group, if you will come and be one for mine." This is a low cost way to get new ideas. (It works best if the guest is from another community, preferably at some distance.)

If you are near a metropolitan area, check the phone book for used book and magazine stores. They can be a good source of used paperbacks and magazines. We were able to get all of Malcolm Boyd's paperback books of prayers for 25 cents each, and of course we bought all the copies they had! Get to know the clerk or the owner of the store; let them know the kinds of things you are interested in. They will often keep an eye out for you.

GRAB-BAG RESOURCE KIT FOR RETREATS

A number of items can be collected and kept together to be ready to go at a moment's notice. These materials can be used for program items and can also be available during free time and schedule transitions, such as just before and after meals. People can discover themselves and their God-given creativity, and contribute to the group.

SUGGESTED STARTING ITEMS (You will come up with many more based on your experiences):

many colors/lots of construction paper	paper sacks
paint: tempera + psychedelic brushes	table games/puzzles
paper/Styrofoam cups	old hats/clothes/wigs/
baby-food jars	broom/mop/simple makeup
clay/Play Doh	

crayons
small scissors
old iron
wax paper
aluminum foil

balloons
large candles
small candles/one for each person
incense

pencils: regular, colored

egg cartons

old magazines/newspapers

pieces of felt + scraps of material
thread

string/wire
telephone wire: many bright
    colors *inside*

Q-tips
toothpicks
straightedge razor blades

paste
glue
sponges
paper towels

pipe cleaners

plaster of paris

masking tape
cellophane tape

scratch paper
newsprint

felt-tip pens (many colors)

Be aware of the NATURAL resources available in your retreat setting: rocks for painting or to use as gifts to each other, twigs, leaves, etc. RECYCLE the dead environment and give it NEW LIFE!

Rich Wagner

HEAVILY USED RESOURCES FOR FINDING PROGRAM ELEMENTS

In looking at all the resources in print, one can soon be flooded under. Here are several kinds of materials which we and others have found useful.

Respond, Volumes 1, 2, 3, and *4.* These volumes are collections of materials, primarily by theme area, which have been created and used by youth leaders and pastors. Each book is organized by section, each section containing a number of actual program outlines and materials. Selected section headings include: Resources for Study and Action—exploring the Word of God, the church, ecology, meditation, politics, Eastern religions, sexuality, international mission, meeting personal needs, vocation; Celebration resources; Handles for leaders/youth and adults; Resources. Other sections scattered through the four volumes include Hymns and Songs; Retreats; and Simulation Games. Volume 3 contains the Index to Volumes 1–3, and Volume 4 contains an Index for all four volumes.

Recycle and *Scan* are companion publications edited by Dennis Benson. They are NOT merely periodicals; they are the sharing organs for hundreds of creative Christian educators throughout the world.

Recycle contains ideas for finding new communication/teaching/worship ideas and uses for items you already have, for example, balloons, salt, the creed, old storage rooms, thermostats, and the like. Created and used by many people, the ideas are summarized, including the name and address of each contributor. If you want an outline/summary or more information on an item, you are encouraged to write, enclosing a self-addressed stamped envelope. GREAT material is recycled for the price of postage.

You may already have a number of ideas/programs which you could recycle!

Scan is a review, again by local folks, of NEW things on the market: books, records, films, tapes, media equipment, etc.

Join the community. Don't keep your ideas to yourself!

Dennis Benson's *Recycle Catalogue* includes 700 ideas for learning, fellowship, mission, and celebration.

The Serendipity Books, by Lyman Coleman, are one of the best sources we have found for small-group exercises, relational Bible study sessions, and in-depth inductive Bible studies. There are twelve books:

for YOUTH—*Man Alive/Kaleidoscope
        Rap* and *Acts Alive;*
for ALL AGES— *Serendipity/Discovery
        Breaking Free/Celebration;*
for SPECIAL USES—*Beginnings/Coffee House Itch
        Festival* (film) *Groups in Action*

Each of the books is divided into three tracks; each track contains material/exercises for six one-hour sessions.

The first track of each book includes material aimed at group building through the sharing of personal history, the affirmation of the strengths and gifts of each member, and the sharing/ministering to the inner needs of each person.

The second track in most books provides six relational Bible study exercises to provide for interaction with the

Scriptures on a personal level and thereby yield personal growth and maturity in Christ.

The third track provides material for six sessions of depth sharing in inductive Bible study based on the latest concepts in Bible study and group dynamics. Leading questions help you make personal and social applications and enable the group-sharing process.

A group can choose to use the material in one of several ways, going track by track one at a time, or moving back and forth between tracks, depending on the maturity/growth of the group.

These materials are NOT a substitute for all the group-building elements which were discussed earlier. They are a resource whose use is determined by YOUR particular goals. They can be used by groups with little group history as a *means* for growth, sharing, building group communi-ty, and communion.

Lyman Coleman also writes a regular column, "Ideas for Groups," in the bimonthly magazine, *Faith/at/Work.* The column features many additional ideas, often in-cluding activities for board planning sessions, teachers' training, and general study and growth groups.

Structured Experiences in Human Relations Training are five volumes of group exercises and games which have been widely used by Christian educators and retreaters! A sampling of group exercises includes: consensus seeking, life planning, the NASA game, problem-solving exer-cises, and many more. Basic instructions, charts, etc., are provided which can be readily adapted for use by church groups.

The *Discovery Series* is a collection of books, each of which includes edited materials arranged by subjects: communication, freedom, love, happiness, peace, and life. The nine student books include:

Discovery in: Prayer, Word, Song, Service, Press,
    Art, Literature, Politics, and *Advertising.*
Teachers' materials include five books: *Discovery in: Drama, Service, Film, Sight,* and *Sign;* plus there are three manuals dealing with the overall philosophy and coordination of the series. Enough material is provided for a three- or four-year course on the Christian, his growth and relationship to other Christians and the world.

You might want to start your collection with *Discovery in Prayer, Word,* and *Song.*

Concern Series, by the Silver Burdett Company, is a very reasonably priced set of Christian education discus-sion materials for teenage students. The booklets are 50 to 60 pages long, each centered upon a single theme:

poverty, race, violence, drugs, revolution, freedom, generation gap, communication, destiny, authority, world religions, and extremists—left and right. The contemporary multicolored layout with many pictures, art illustrations, and collages adds to their appeal. A leader's guide to the whole series contains general suggestions on how to lead a discussion group, film and resource ideas, and a lengthy section of discussion questions for each chapter of each of the student books.

Youth Specialties is the source of *Ideas,* Volumes I–16. *Ideas* includes material collected from youth workers and is arranged by categories: crowd breakers, games, special events, publicity and promotion, creative communica-tion, skits and dramatics, multimedia, camping, and prizes. Not every section is included in each book, but most are. They are expensive, but useful.

The Wittenburg Door is a bimonthly publication of Youth Specialties which contains satire, articles, and resources of use to workers with youth. Some experimen-tal films are available through them also.

A number of retreat programs have been based on the Argus Communications' Choose Life Series. Like the Discovery Series, and the Serendipity Series, these materials could be used by a high school or young-adult group for several years. Combinations of media, films, records, posters, and taped documentaries are used to reach and motivate today's teens. On the whole, the series seems to be more discussion oriented as opposed to the more interpersonal/relational group-growth focus of the *Serendipity* books. You will have to choose/integrate resources on the basis of your goals and preferences.

The series is divided into three sets of four books: *first:* awareness, life-cycle, signs of the times, and ultimate concern. *Second:* people, signs and symbols, change, freedom. *Third:* community, promise, faith, and social concern. Each book contains twenty detailed lesson plans and ideas on each subject.

MEDIA RESOURCES

Access to audiovisual equipment is valuable for any group. If you do not have use of the items suggested below, check with other churches in your area. Suggest sharing, renting, or even joint purchase. Videotape can often be borrowed from schools, mental-health departments, or businesses in the community.

Useful items are: movie projectors (16 mm and Super-8); a portable record player and tape players; Super-8 movie camera; posters; black light; strobe; slide projector; supplies to make your own slides; Instamatic or 35 mm cameras—the list is endless. See the List of Resources for specific "how-to-do-it" books in media, and the Appendix for retreat media program ideas.

FILM RESOURCES

Check with your area schools, libraries, and service clubs for free films. For example, Pennsylvania has a statewide free film library system with over 7,000 films. Also, nearly one-fourth of the Mass Media Ministries' catalog selection is available free to Pennsylvania residents.

Sources of films and reviews of them are endless. A complete listing of sources, and many reviews can be found in the current edition of the *Audio-Visual Resource Guide.* Instead of purchasing this volume right away, for free catalogs, using church stationery, write to some of the sources listed in this book and in the bibliographies of the books listed in the List of Resources, such as *Respond.* A list of heavily used films is included in the List of Resources.

MUSICAL RESOURCES

Check out the talents of the group. Who plays what? Who is interested in learning to play the guitar? Find someone to teach a small group, and next year you will have your own "in-house" music.

Does your group have a song sheet or book, either one which they have compiled themselves, or one which is

purchased? Making one is not hard, and new favorites can be added each year.

Commercial songbooks which can be used include: *Songs: Hymnal for Young Christians* (F.E.L.), volumes 1 and 2; and *Songs for Celebration.* Check the List of Resources and your local Christian bookstore.

Encourage your group members to bring their own musical instruments or to make their own—guitars, ukes, whistles, recorders, bones, Autoharps, pans, bottles, sandpaper blocks. Use your imagination!

Records and contemporary music can be readily used in programming and worship experiences. You might have a "favorites" night with discussion centering on the "message" of each cut in light of the Christian faith. Check the contents of *Songs,* the record index in *Ventures in Worship,* the *Media Source-book* and your Christian bookstore.

CREATIVE-EXPERIMENTAL WORSHIP RESOURCES

In addition to material included in the Appendix and List of Resources, refer to the material and bibliography in *Ventures in Worship,* volume 3. Lists include annotated information on books, periodicals; insight on celebrative activity; art, banners, posters, photography; drama; dance; music, records, hymnals, songbooks; liturgy, words, and cassettes.

CRAFT RESOURCES

Special opportunities for creative expression can be made available as part of the program and free time. It is best to have persons who know what they are doing supervise each activity, organize the material, keep track of it, and collect any money charged to help pay for resources.

Potential areas are as endless as your imagination, resource people, and group interests. Some possibilities are making group mobiles, macrame, tie-dying, candle making, leather work, and banner making. Consider, also, jewelry and enameling, pottery or ceramics, using a portable wheel and kiln; sculpture and welding—every community has a welder, invite him/her and the family along, with portable gear, of course.

RECREATIONAL RESOURCES

Always check with the facility you will be using to see what is available. Their supply can be supplemented: Frisbees, Wiffle balls, bats, hoola-hoops; Nerf balls; Super balls; Tinker-Toys; plastic construction sets;

puzzles; M.E.M.E.; football; and other standard items. Many active indoor games for individuals or small groups can be purchased or made after ideas from World Wide Games. We generally have not found youth interested in playing long games while on retreats (Monopoly, etc.). The most popular items have been ones which demand some mental/physical skill and which can be picked up or put down easily.

SPECIAL READING RESOURCES FOR YOUTH; THE READING GRAB BAG

We encourage youth to read, anything, just read. Many have not learned to read well in school and have a negative attitude toward trying. Anything they do in this area we praise. We do not provide copies of questionable material, but we usually do not confiscate it if it shows up. (See discussion of this point on pp. 24-25.)

We DO encourage youth to bring their magazines, for example, *Mad* and comic books. Comics in the last five to ten years have become increasingly "theological" in dealing with the struggle between good/evil, etc. *Mad*

particularly offers many ideas and resources for discussion, program input, and skits. Some of the subject areas from *Mad, Peanuts,* and other cartoon strips include attitudes on: dating, boy-girl relationships; parent-teen communication, generation gap; TV/movie satire; politics; social problems; prejudice; and many others.

The most notable use of *Mad* in a specifically theological way is *The Mad Morality: Or the Ten Commandments Revisited.* (All the *Mad* pocket books can be part of the book resource bag.)

The Gospel According to Peanuts is another good example of comics being used to discuss theological questions. You can do this YOURSELF. Read the comics; cut and save those strips which hit you. Several that we cut from regularly include "Peanuts," "B.C.," "Winthrop," "Tumbleweeds," "Wizard of Id," "Eek and Meek," "Short Ribs," "Sgt. Stripes Forever," and "Doonsbury." Start your collection today. Throw them all into a folder, and then go through it when you are compiling program resources. If your paper doesn't carry any of these comics, write to the owner and suggest these titles.

Paperback books are also available, including collections of cartoons from: "B.C," "Wizard of Id," "Peanuts," "Wee Pals," "Mad," etc.

Humor in general is a great source of program material. Check out the humor/comedy record albums at the record shop, and ask your group about their favorites. (Cosby, Vaughn Meader, Lear, Fire-Side Theater, *et al.*)

ORGANIZING RESOURCES FOR USE DURING THE RETREAT

In making resources available to the retreat participants, we found it easiest to separate the various activities, using a table for each. There usually are a couple of book tables, one with puzzles and games, another with tapes, tape recorders, media stuff, paints, and crafts. All of these we want easily accessible, and we try to have them in heavy traffic areas, especially the books, so that people will read/use them while waiting for dinner. Some tables will need to be in an area where they can be locked up for the night or during times when they are not in use. This of course depends on the nature of the facility, who else is using it, and related factors.

Have all the possibilities for resources exhausted you? We hope not. This whole area is one for continuing ingenuity, creativity, and one through which individuals can express their feelings for God and each other.

Turn to the List of Resources for each category, and for suggestions as to which items to purchase if you are just beginning to collect resources for your groups.

10. The Schedule

THE PROGRAM IS GIVEN LIFE IN TIME AND SPACE BY THE *SCHEDULE*. Answering when, where, in what order, and for how long each program element will occur is the task of the schedule.

To decide these timing and spatial questions, one needs to consider:

1. the primary goal and the time needs of the essential program elements
2. the total length of time available
3. the spatial layout of the facility
4. the length of travel time needed
5. the time needed for daily eating, sleeping
6. who is participating (age, age range, experience, and total number)
7. other time considerations for DOING the retreat.

HARMONY BETWEEN SCHEDULE AND PROGRAM AND GOAL

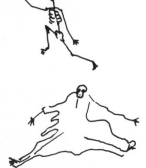

Picture a skeleton with fewer muscles than bones. Many of the bones would hang useless and rattle. Now picture a skeleton with far too few bones for the amount of musculature. It would be hard to get up off the ground.

Muscle and bones function together for movement toward a goal much as program and schedule do. The schedule skeleton can be cumbersome or too scanty for exciting implementation of program. Schedules (like programs) need to be tailored to the goal and the resources chosen to reach that goal. A group needs to clarify the goal or goals, then build the schedule and program to meet that goal.

The scheduling elements that vary according to the goals of the retreat tend to be: the amount of free time; the amount of structured recreation; the amount of alone time; the proportion of time spent in small groups, large groups, worship, and formal learning sessions; the amount of silence; the amount of physical activity versus quiet action; the amount of expressive and creative time; the amount of sleep and eating time.

TOTAL LENGTH OF TIME

Schedules can range from one day apart to a week or longer trip. The length of time for retreating may be determined by outside considerations, such as other competing commitments, tight schedules, or precedence. It is ideal when the length of time is determined by assessing the amount of time needed to achieve substantial movement toward the goal. Planning ahead can sometimes be a way to clear the amount of time needed for the retreat.

The longer the total time to be spent, the larger will be the number of program elements which can feasibly be included, and more consideration needs to be given to the pacing of activity. People can maintain high intensity thought or pure play for short periods of time, but they need breaks if either extreme is to be sustained over long periods of time.

THE PLACE SPACE

The amount of time invested in settling into a place and "making it ours" varies according to the length of time to be spent at that location. A moving retreat makes its *place* the vehicle of transportation, rest stops, and sleeping spots. Time needs to be scheduled for "relocation activities." More time may be needed if the facility calls for bringing a lot from home or if it invites sports equipment.

The type of space which your facility provides can influence how many activities can be scheduled at once. Are there private spots for small group meetings or a stay-up room away from sleepers? How much do you have to cater to the predetermined schedule of the facility for meals, recreation, and lights-out? Will other groups need to be sharing your space?

LENGTH OF TRAVEL TIME

When the length of travel time is long in comparison to the total retreat time, the traveling activity itself should be tailored so that it becomes focused program time. If this is difficult, it may be wise to select a closer location.

DAILY LIVING ACTIVITIES

There is a tendency to get locked into a view of time determined by the ordinary timing of five events: rising, breakfast, lunch, dinner, and retiring. This structure yields three large time blocks for developing program.

We have found that some altering of the basic-five frame can prove workable to enhance some retreat goals.

1. *Variations on bedtime.* To utilize the energy and excitement (especially but not solely the property of youth) on the first night of retreating, several options have been tried successfully:
   a. "Stay-Up" area away from those who want to sleep, with program resources and leader available, and with a maximum late hour. Quite a few meaningful discussions occur in this setting.
   b. "All-Nighter" as part of the program, converting what is ordinarily spent in whispering, wakeful "sleep" into conscious program time. Sleep is then scheduled for the next day.
   c. "Late Night" the first night until 4:00 A.M. with rising scheduled at 11:00 A.M., with the next evening's lights-out scheduled at 1:00 A.M. to ease transition back to ordinary schedule.

Whatever alteration of sleep time is made, it should be understood by all that each person is responsible for participating in the planned activities during the retreat and for not giving excuses upon return home for not being able to carry out responsibilities of school or work.

Many adults find these alterations in bedtime very exhausting; the benefits seem to be primarily for youth. Adult leaders on youth retreats should be given adequate time for rest; otherwise leadership quality goes down.

2. *Arising time.* Scheduling activity in the early morning can be difficult to implement, especially with youth. Even giving clever titles to early morning activities does not always overcome the resistance surrounding rising. There are bound to be both night-people and day-people with you. If the planning committee would like to utilize this early morning time, make it optional with suggested focus.

Scheduling optional activities in locations away from sleepers at both ends of the day makes scheduling and leadership needs a bit more complex. However, it may well be worth maximizing on different persons' rhythms of energy.

3. *Clues about mealtime.* Varying the number of meals a day or having a fasting retreat can offer opportunity for different timing of major programming. (The breaks which meals provide are still needed!) Meals may be able to be timed for responsiveness to what is going on in the program. This is most feasible when the group is doing its own cooking. It is possible that an agreement for a "waitable" meal may be made with the cooks. Some groups have handled the need for flexible worship time by planning a snack during the service and holding dinner off until a later hour.

In scheduling time for daily activities, remember also that people need time to dress, wash, go to the bathroom, and to be alone DAILY. Schedule such personal time IN!

WHO IS ON THE RETREAT? People!

Consider the *balance* and *demand* of your total schedule. Each element may be terrific in and of itself, but put them all together and only super people could keep up with the demand on energy!

Pruning the schedule for pace and activity level may be in order, so that people do not return from the retreat utterly exhausted (parents especially become critical). The demand level may well be higher than daily life because the retreat is a time-out for concentrating on certain goals, but be aware of the tendency to pack too much in when planning. However, to schedule too much and then cut is preferable to being caught short with not enough to do and a very bored group.

The age and age span of the people participating influences schedule needs. Obviously senior citizens have different energy levels and attention spans than junior high youth. One general rule of thumb is: the focused attention span of a person equals his age in minutes up to a maximum of 25 minutes.

For examples of schedules appropriate to different age groups see in Appendix:

Junior Highs: 23—open time periods with short sections of focused time

24—lots of input and changes in pace

Older Youth: 39—three program sections plus worship and optional programming

Adult: 43, 52, 53—increased proportion of focused time

Mixed Ages: 49—lots of options; short chunks of time

45—different activities and times

Effective retreats have been held for varying time periods during a weekend:

1. starting Friday mid-evening; going to mid-afternoon Sunday
2. starting late Friday evening (9–10), leaving at noon on Sunday
3. starting Saturday afternoon at 2:00 and closing Sunday afternoon at 2:00
4. starting Saturday morning; closing late afternoon Saturday

OTHER SCHEDULE CONSIDERATIONS

On almost every retreat, time needs to be scheduled for:

arrival and orientation,

closing and evaluation,

free time for everyone,

leaders' meetings,

transition from one activity to another.

Smoothness in moving from one program element to another can be increased by:

1. Having copies of suggested schedule for all
   or
   posting large-sized copies of schedule.
2. Designating certain people as "convenors" to give 5-minute warnings before a change in activity.
3. Using a fun noisemaker to signal times for change. It is sometimes helpful to have an external object rather than a person be the "interrupter."
4. Having one person take full responsibility for time keeping and flow. (In one retreat each participant was required to place his wristwatch in a basket and trust the leader.)

SCHEDULE POWER

Your group's attitude toward the function of a schedule can be discussed and agreed upon ahead of time. If one of the goals of the retreat is for participants to learn greater discipline, then a very close following of the schedule, despite unpredictable elements, may be decided upon. With any other goal, a military following of the schedule can deny the presence of the Holy Spirit and can work against the goals which the schedule was created to enable.

The schedule may be A SUGGESTED FRAMEWORK,

A MEASURING ROD;

BUT IT IS NOT GOD.

There are problems with being flexible: changing the schedule takes time; confusion may be experienced during the change; one might have to leave out something of potential value that had been planned. However, being flexible allows for RESPONSE to changing awarenesses, needs, and emerging goals.

> "The sabbath was made for man, not man for the sabbath" (Mark 2:27).

11. Leadership

The number and kinds of leadership needs and functions will vary depending on the kind of retreat being planned and the kind of program envisioned.

Possible leaders by function:

1. general coordinator.
2. program leaders: outside special persons or local people with special training or skills,

   small group leaders,

   schedule-coordinator.
3. general counselors for living groups.
4. people with special skills additional to main programming: for example, music, cooking, recreation, lifesaving, crafts, media, resource-gatherer.
5. people with no assigned responsibilities other than to observe, keep an overview, help handle emergencies.

HOW MANY LEADERS ARE ENOUGH?

The major factors varying the ratio of leaders to participants will be related to WHO is going and what are the GOALS. If there is a mixture of races, cultural subgroups, and ages who don't know one another, then there will need to be more leaders. If the youth are "juvenile delinquents," "emotionally disturbed," or have serious health problems, then an increase in leadership is necessary. The ratio may even approach one to two or one to one in some cases.

On adult retreats there may only be one or two persons responsible for the program—perhaps one outside person for presentations and one inside person to handle group maintenance functions, convene sessions, and coordinate the schedule. Depending on the goals, the program, and how the food is being handled, there may be need for more leaders.

The average youth group can function with an adult leadership/participant ratio of anywhere from one to four to one to eight. One adult for every five or six youth is a good compromise. It is good to have both men and women in leadership capacities, even for a small group.

Having a larger number of adult leaders allows for more opportunity for adult/youth dialogue and interaction. It allows for dealing with individual problems while the group continues in its task or program. It allows for someone to deal with emergencies without using the basic group leaders.

It is *possible* to conduct retreats with one adult for fifteen youth or more. This should be attempted—

1. when the leaders know and have worked with each other and the group previously;
2. when the youth know each other, work well together, and have demonstrated ability to plan, execute, and assume responsibility.

Can there ever be too many leaders? YES, when—

1. the number of adults overwhelms the youth (subjective feeling);
2. the number of leaders is not worth the problem of keeping them coordinated;
3. there are not enough jobs to do and the leaders feel uncomfortable without specific responsibility;
4. the leaders cannot agree on basics.

WHERE AND HOW TO FIND RETREAT LEADERS

Potential leaders for working with youth can be found in and through any intergenerational activity where adults and youth have a chance to get to know one another as real people. One pastor resisted organizing a church softball team for several months, thinking of it as "one more activity." However, through the team three couples emerged as youth advisers over a period of two years. Plan and encourage intergenerational activities!

Bud Carroll and Keith Ignatius suggest *visiting* the people who are being asked to have a leadership role on the retreat.[1] Telephoning is far less personal. Ask several youth to go visiting with you to call on potential leaders and counselors. The youth can also be a source of suggestions for names.

[1] John L. Carroll and Keith L. Ignatius, *Youth Ministry: Sunday, Monday, and Every Day* (Valley Forge: Judson Press, 1972), chapter 3.

Be fair with those whom you have recruited to serve on the retreat. Do not expect them to take continuing leadership of the group just because they had a good weekend. You may want to approach the person(s) later to ask them to consider further leadership responsibility. However, beware of pressuring. They can be approached another year if they are not turned off the first time.

YOUTH are potential leaders for working with younger youth. This can work well if the older youth are mature and are given a clear understanding of what is expected of them. Responsibilities can be geared to the capacity of these youth leaders.

There is some risk in this approach. Some youth may be tempted to "use the group" or live through it to act out his/her own rebellion or fantasies. An identity conflict may develop within the youth leader between his/her need for acceptance by the group and his/her need to function as an enforcer of ground rules. Another risk is that the older youth may "take over" the smaller groups, thus shrinking the younger ones' opportunity for growth. *These temptations are there for adults, too;* AGE is not the only criterion for maturity!

Despite the risks, there are a lot of benefits in using older youth as leaders:

1. The younger youth have someone nearer their own age to emulate.
2. The younger youth experience the caring of people who have more status in school.
3. The older youth can identify with the group and may be able to sense what is relevant and of interest for ideas for programs.
4. The older youth have a chance to develop leadership skills.

PREPARATION FOR THE RETREAT

1. *Clear Division of Labor.* Job descriptions and expectations need to be determined well in advance, especially if the person has planning responsibilities for the retreat itself. A planning coordinator should work with each person or task force to establish specific target dates for completing their task. (Always allow at least one extra week in setting the deadline.)

Not checking in advance of the deadline can be embarrassing—two days until the retreat and no menus! By checking well in advance, the coordinator can help the person confront his/her own lack of action, clarify what needs to be done, secure more help, or if necessary, find someone else to handle the responsibility.

If a leader finds himself/herself overburdened and unable to carry out a particular area of responsibility, encourage feedback and possible revision of the preplanned division of labor. (Leaders with heavy program responsibilities often find themselves unable to be available and helpful as living-group counselors.)

During the retreat people need to know to whom to take problems or questions.

2. *Leaders' Meetings.* One, or several, leaders' meetings BEFORE the retreat are helpful in getting acquainted and in building a supportive team spirit. This is important even if the leaders know one another and have worked together before because people may change even in a short period of time. A lack of unity in spirit, trust, or caring can invite the group to divide and play off leaders against one another.

Any "extra" adults who will be going (for transportation) could attend the meetings in order to get an overview and to prevent misunderstanding and possible spread of misinformation.

Invite and give opportunity for feedback.

In addition to clarifying the division of labor, pre-retreat leadership discussion should include:

a. prayer
b. clarification of goals (purposes)
c. review of who is going
d. review of past retreats' strengths and weaknesses
e. review of mechanics of group life: transportation, food preparation, program elements, facilities, schedule, resources
f. discussion of group rules:
—what participants can decide
—process for dealing with problems
g. asking for and receiving help, support from one another.

3. *Update.* Leaders need to be kept up to date with any changes or exceptions to policy, ground rules, program, schedule, etc., in order to do premium quality teamwork. This sharing of information contributes to smoothness in operation and enhanced trust. Lack of such information lowers morale. If at all possible, leaders should be involved or consulted for any major changes.

4. *Time Off.* See that each leader has at least one major block of time *completely* free during the retreat. It is preferable to have some time off each day, but this is not always possible. If this break is not built into the leaders' expectations, patience can wear thin, minor problems can escalate, and the general tension level can increase.

Rich Wagner

Leaders who come home exhausted and have to spend a day or so recuperating may not be as likely to help out again. They may also discourage friends from going.

5. *Pause to Gather.* Schedule time for leaders to meet at least once during the retreat (preferably once a day) to check in with one another. This provides opportunity for prayer, fellowship, and sharing about specific situations, individuals, or problems. Evaluate; make needed changes; support one another. You will find that this short "apart-time" can render you more *available* to retreat participants.

Extra. An extra aid provided to leaders by some enablers has been a written leaders' guide sheet sum-marizing goals, philosophy, schedule, program respon-sibilities, "how tos," and sensitizing suggestions.

PLAN TO TAKE CARE OF YOUR LEADERS.
Be aware of their needs as people:
for support,   for strokes,   for breathers,
for permission to make mistakes,
for recognition.

Energy spent in preparing leaders for the retreat is WELL spent; for it is through PEOPLE—open and trusting—that God's love and truth are revealed.

12. Ground Rules

Why have ground rules? Many would say, "To protect the participants and others from harm." The harm might be physical, emotional, legal, financial, social, or spiritual. Ground rules serve not only as a *keeping from* arrangement but also as a structure to *move toward* responsible behavior and expression of caring for self and others.

It is through ground rules that we make clear to one another what we expect of ourselves and them, what our limits are, and what our values are. Determining ground rules can be an opportunity in a Christian setting to reflect on values and consequences of human behavior.

Ground rules are most helpful when they come from the *ground* we experience as Christians:

> GOD expressing himself
> through Christ
> to persons.

"You must love the Lord your God with all your heart, with all your soul, and with all your mind. . . . You must love your neighbor as yourself" (Matthew 22:37-39).

"We love, because he first loved us" (1 John 4:19, RSV).

"By this all men will know that you are my disciples, if you have love for one another" (John 13:35, RSV).

Ground rules also very much need to be grounded in the decisions about goals of the retreat and the type of schedule and program needed to accomplish the goals. Fun and fellowship retreats may need fewer ground rules regarding boundaries and required participation than highly structured cognitive or experiential retreats. Ground rules can provide a framework for choices that will discourage sidetracks and will point participants toward finding the most in their retreat experience.

WHO DECIDES?

The more people involved in developing the ground rules for the retreat, the more time-consuming the

By permission of John Hart and Field Enterprises, Inc.

planning becomes, but also the more the group OWNS the rules rather than just AGREEing to them.

EXAMPLE: When four seventh grade boys were found in a girls' cabin at 3:00 in the afternoon, one leader "blew up" and ordered the boys be sent home. The leader had NOT honestly shared his strong feelings about the ground rule which limited visitation by opposite sex to before 6 P.M. When this leader's choice of consequence was NOT selected or enforced by the director, the leader packed up his car and drove home.

If a small group develops the ground rules, it is crucial to allow for discussion, integration, and time change by the large group. This may not be necessary in depth for every retreat of an ongoing group once a precedent has been set. (However, see Retreat Disaster, chapter 3.)

The "enabled-participation" style of leadership is valuable in decision making about ground rules. There may be many situations where group decision making of the ground rules is impractical or unwise, and in these cases the leaders would take the responsibility:

1. When the retreat group is large (over 30) with no previous history.
2. When the group gathering for the retreat is varied in cultural backgrounds, with no history as a group.
3. When the group is made up of people weak in valuing others and sometimes themselves (for example, deprived or discriminated-against people).
4. When the retreat needs to be planned in a hurry for specific goals not emphasizing personal growth in decision making.
5. When the group has always been leader directed and does not want to change.
6. If the group is making "way-out" decisions that would potentially threaten the existence of the group or members.

In some of these cases the leaders may choose to let the group decide and force them to accept and deal with the consequences. Such a decision is putting the goal of the group learning from this one experience far above any other goal if the existence of the group is at stake.

Staging. It is *possible* to move a group toward greater responsibility for its own code of behavior.

> Self-direction is *desirable*
> because ultimately each of
> us is responsible before
> God for our choices.

Self-direction is *practical,* for it is harder to break "my rules" or "our rules" than "their rules."

The progression may not be easy due to the many forces in society which are set up for governing behavior externally. There is also perhaps a universal tendency to blame others for one's responsibility—teachers saying, "The problem of this child comes from the home," and parents saying, "If the school and church were doing their jobs, my child would be better."

The movement from externally directed rules to internally directed ones can look like this:

1. Handle decisions about ground rules among leaders and with the individuals who have broken the ground rules.
2. Delegate to participants minor areas for decision making so that mistakes are not far-reaching or too destructive (for example, who comes on retreat).
3. Use a United Nations' model with leaders being the security council with veto power and the general assembly coming up with proposals on all issues.
4. Have leaders function as *initiators* and *guides* as the group decides and enforces all ground rules.

WHO ENFORCES? "Cops and Robbers," Anyone?

It is exhausting to be an investigating agent or the "heavy." Why not share the responsibility, in fact, transform the game from "Cops and Robbers" to CARING? If participants are aware of, have agreed with, or perhaps *own* the ground rules, then expectations of acceptable behavior infuse the atmosphere. The limits and possibilities are known to all as a guide for the retreat experience.

If and when an expectation is violated, there are several suggestions for deciding who handles the problem:
1. one-to-one peer
2. a small group of peers fact-finding and administering consequences
3. the counselor who discovers the breach
4. the primary leaders or director
5. an arbitration team made up of leaders and participants
6. the large group dealing with breaches
7. when it is a family retreat—
   a. biological parents
   b. persons delegated in charge of children
   c. group discussion
   d. the whole program focus.

We have used several of these models successfully. We usually let the groups know that we always expect peer action. For minor breaches we have had the immediate counselor make the decision. For larger offenses we have most often used an arbitration team composed of director, counselor, and *the youth involved in the breach*. The incident can become a teachable moment. We have also brought issues back to the whole group for discussion, role playing, and development of consequences.

Note: Ground rules may be broken by *adults* as well. This discussion of ways to handle breaches applies to all ages.

For major offenses, peer handling alone is unacceptable not only because leaders have responsibility and a stake in the future of the group, but also because they are accountable to the church for what happens.

Whatever model or combination of models you choose, it is best to PUBLICIZE that choice to participants before the retreat.

WHAT GROUND RULES ARE NEEDED?

There is no end to the number and kind of problems which may arise in a person's behavior. That is the wonder and beauty of our diversity as individual creatures of God. However, some common problem areas can be anticipated.

Issues to be decided upon for ANY RETREAT are:
1. Who is going?
2. Who is responsible for what?
3. What amount of participation in program and schedule is required?
4. What are the spatial and time limits (boundaries)?
5. Who sleeps where; what groupings are inviolate?
6. In-group/out-group conflict.

For YOUTH retreats, these issues are also important:
7. Abuse of personal standards or self:
   a. drugs
   b. sex
   c. eating
   d. sleep
8. Hurting others:
   a. stealing
   b. destroying property
   c. unfair fighting
   d. lying
   e. sexual intercourse
   f. invasion of privacy

Getting Started. One very natural place to start determining ground rules with youth is to ask "What is a reasonable time for everyone to be in bed?" Discuss the alternatives possible. This is often an issue of lively interest. For other groups the question may be asked, "What ground rules do we need to accomplish the goals of

this retreat?" The group will need to look at the givens: Are the people who are going searching or settled in their value system? What are the outside expectations upon the retreat group: of parents, of the home church, of the facility to be used, of the legal system in society? In general, the group will need to comply with the major expectations of the groups within which it operates or else be prepared to spend time defending, educating, or working out the repercussions.

If the group is a youth group, the ground rules issued may be extremely important. Teens are the years in which people experiment with life-style. Many teens come from restrictive families and will want to use the "away" opportunity to explore new behavior, challenging parental rule while out from under the thumb. Some young people have never been away from home or have never lived in a communal situation and so are not aware of appropriate or inappropriate behavior. Many are floundering and looking for some guidelines.

Perhaps adults may want or need room for values clarification. (We often assume that by adulthood people have decided where they stand on many issues.) In any age group, there are those who prefer the external structure and input, and those who desire a more flexible schedule and rules in order to experiment with their values and life-style.

Should consequences of broken ground rules be stated? There are pros and cons. Explicit statement does give people fair warning. However, it often works better to leave unsaid what specific consequence will follow what action because—
1. handling each situation in an individual fashion seems to be most meaningful for that individual's change process;
2. talking about the *results* of broken rules often tends to invite the fulfillment of expectations.

For exceptions, where the offense was repeated by some of the same people, see discussion of drugs, in chapter 23 where the development of the process of handling problems is found.

EXPRESSING GROUND RULES

We like to see ground rules expressed positively: "thou shalts," rather than "thou shalt nots." However, stating the negatives may be briefer and clearer, for they set definite limits.

Whether written down or expressed orally, it is important for all retreaters to be informed of the ground rules.

One way of presenting the rules is to use a covenant to be signed as people register for the retreat. For example:

I, _____, do COVENANT to
   participate in all planned events,
   carry my share of responsibility,
   sing and make noise and celebrate now and
   then,
   experiment with new ways of being myself
      and relating to people and to God,
   take care of my body,
   do daring, loving things for others,
   take care of the place,
   let the leaders know if and for how long
      I need to leave this community.
                              Signed,

Developing and handling problems with ground
rules can be an expression of love
providing stakes
for people's growth
toward the SOURCE.

Lynn Nelson

13. Location and Facilities

Location and facilities should be considered in light of the goals for the retreat. For example, a group-building retreat would have difficulty if there were no small, private, group meeting rooms or no room large enough for the whole group. The primitiveness of the cooking area may mean that a lot of valuable time is used for cooking and not for other group goals. The way the sleeping facilities are arranged could increase closeness or increase feelings of privateness or even separation. The recreational lure may prove a hearty distraction from a retreat which is supposed to be primarily task oriented.

Selection of facilities should also take into account the age and preferences of the people who are going. Many adults may not like to crowd ten to a room for sleeping; youth may enjoy it. Some do not like roughing it out-of-doors; others enjoy the challenge of a primitive facility. Family groups who want to sleep together may find that camping or trailering is the most convenient way to go. If the purpose of the retreat is for people of different cultural groups to get to know one another, a facility which could house small sleeping groups would be ideal.

LOW-COST LOCATIONS

Before selecting a site, *consider the alternatives.* There are high-cost plans and low-cost ones. Low-cost plans include:

1. Use your own church. Disadvantages to this plan are: it is not a place "away" and so considered "less special"; it is more difficult to keep the boundaries (temptation for those within to communicate with those without).
2. Use another church across town. This provides a somewhat new setting; hence it's more special.
3. Have one night at the church and the other away at camp or conference grounds.
4. Stay at the home of someone in your church. Tim Peterson, while pastoring in New Jersey, opened his house for a junior high "one-nighter" each month. A couple in our church offered their summer house in Maine as a retreat location. Private homes, unless large and subdivided, may be less appropriate for adult

or family groups than for youth who enjoy more crowding and less privacy.
5. Tent in public or private campgrounds (reserve adjoining sites for large groups) or on someone's farm.
6. Exchange room and board for service. Such arrangements are available in inner cities, in Appalachia, on Indian reservations, in Mexico and other countries, and of course at many local church camp and conference centers.
7. Use other sites: youth hostels, motels at group rates, houseboats, empty freight cars, backpacking into the wilderness.

It is easy to get in a RUT by going to the same place every time. Even if your favorite place is very special, another facility may enhance your program goal in a new way.

HOW TO FIND NEW LOCATIONS

Look over your congregation. Let your need be known. You may have connections right at home.

Ask your minister and other ministers in your area if they know of people with a summer home or campsites which are suited to your needs.

Write various denominational headquarters for lists of their facilities and the range of costs.

Check out Scout or "Y" camps.

Talk to the travel club; get a list of public and private campgrounds.

PLANNING FOR USE OF THE LOCATION

Visit the facility before the retreat, or, if that is not possible, write for a detailed description of the physical structures and grounds so that you can determine its advantages and limitations. Knowing what is available and what you need to bring eliminates many irritating hitches.

Make reservations ahead of time. Some places are booked one or two years in advance. Many states now have reservation procedures for state and county parks. Even when going to another church, allow plenty of time (three or four months) for the request to be considered by their board.

Most, if not all, of these places will want to know:

1. the number of people coming, number of men, number of women, ages;

2. the number of separate sleeping sites needed;

3. the plan for handling meals;

4. the type of meeting and recreation space needed.

It is helpful to obtain written confirmation of your reservation.

LOCATION INFLUENCES PROGRAM

Exciting program ideas can grow from selecting interesting retreat sites:

CASE 1: Upon writing a community minister in New York City requesting lodging in his church for two nights, we received a reply which opened up an opportunity for the retreaters to visit with a number of VISTA workers. Also the minister offered to lead several discussions on topics related to the theme of the retreat.

CASE 2: "The Shared Toilet." On a retreat to Vermont, thirty-three people shared one bathroom which had one toilet and one sink. The gal-primpers got a lot of teasing from fellows waiting in line. The forced sharing of personal duties prompted a closeness, some anger, a mealtime skit, and an eventual cooperation which was rare.

Become aware of locations and facilities which offer unique or popular recreational activities. These sites can help motivate people not yet attracted by other retreat goals. The natural beauty of a location may be truly inspiring. Take these unique features into account and plan time for their enjoyment during the retreat. You can utilize them to enhance your program goals (for example, fellowship and spiritual growth).

Some retreats take the form of a *moving* location: a pack trip into the Sierras; a bike trip between churches in Iowa; a cross-country trip to Florida and then to the Bahamas. (See p. 40.) The moving location becomes itself a part of the major program focus:

broadening one's awareness and base of experience,

encountering nature,

discovering new people and places,

learning and sharing,

witnessing.

ENVIRONMENT HAS POWER. It can pollute or freshen your retreat. Choose to use it to enhance rather than detract from your retreat purpose.

14. Meals

Mealtimes have long been used by retreat goers as part of the program—having prayer before and often having singing, announcements, discussions, or skits immediately afterward. Several other ideas which may enhance your chosen retreat goal are:

1. Eating the meal in a special way:
   —in silence
   —listening to a reading
   or music selected by
   participants
   —without utensils
   with a cameraman
   on hand
   —in the manner of
   another culture

   Goal—personal spiritual growth

   Goal—feeling "at home"
   Goal—pure fun

   Goal—experiential learning

2. Arranging seating in different ways:
   to build small groups,
   to enlarge the circle of friends,
   to focus on a common center.

3. Varying the setting: outdoors, darkness, formal, informal.

4. Having a mealtime simulation game with tables representing different continents and food distributed to tables in proportion to actual food distribution in the world.

5. Fasting and having a service to dedicate money not used for food to go for a specific need elsewhere.

Meals are an opportunity for team building, more so if the group decides to do its own cooking. But even when others are providing the meals, K.P. can be handled not only efficiently but also with purpose and verve!

K.P. DUTIES

The division of labor needed for setting tables, clearing, and cleanup can be handled in several ways.

One way is to have each person take care of his/her own K.P. for each meal. A tub of hot soapy water and a container of hot rinse water are set at each table along with a drainer. Each person scrapes his/her plate, washes, rinses, and places it in the drainer. Before the next meal each one sets his/her own place. This system does eliminate the need for most K.P. committees except for cleaning the pots and pans and the serving dishes.

Another procedure is to form small committees to spend an hour or so doing the K.P. duties for the *whole group* each meal. The committees can be formed by circulating a sign-up sheet with meals listed and the number of people needed. People sign up under the meal of their choice until the committee is full. The times to report for duty need to be stated for each meal.

With an efficient system worked out, the job spread out so that people carry a fairly equal share of the load, and with a brief "reality" approach in presentation, the griping about K.P. is minimal. The cleanup time can even be fun with others hanging around to socialize, tell jokes, sing, or even pitch in out of turn. (A movement toward this spirit can be started by a small minority and it's catching.) Recognition by the group for jobs well done feels great, too.

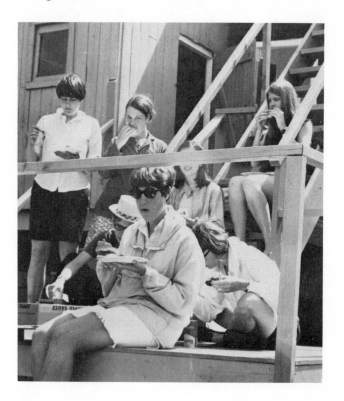

COOKING THE MEALS

There are various ways of providing the meals. Some "cooks" from your church may plan and prepare the meals, or the retreat participants may share in the planning and preparation through a committee organization. Or, the facility where the retreat is held may provide the meal preparation. There are advantages and disadvantages in each approach:

Let the Facility Do the Cooking

Pros	*Cons*
Quick and easy for the group, leaving more time for other program elements.	Little voice in the menu. No recognition of distaste for some foods or menu inappropriate for age group.
Little advanced planning needed.	Little flexibility in meal schedule.
	Lack of appreciation of the work involved.
	Can be expensive.

Delegated Leader "Cooks"

Pros	*Cons*
More freedom for group to do other things.	Group may be unappreciative of work involved.
More choice in menu.	More griping about food choice or way prepared.
Some time flexibility to respond to program needs.	
More likely to be inexpensive.	

Participant Cooking

Pros	*Cons*
More choice in menu.	Takes time and energy to plan.
Some time flexibility.	Takes time from other things during retreat.
More likely to be inexpensive.	May be some "flops" in timing or preparation.
Possibility for "food-griping" youth group to learn a lesson!	
Opportunity for adult retreaters to share the load.	
Opportunity to learn new skills.	
Opportunity to serve one another.	
Opportunity for team building.	

Action Steps. If the group decides to do its own cooking by committee as an expression of program and budgetary goals, the committee will need to do the following planning and implementing of tasks:

1. Plan menus. Select foods for a balanced diet, appropriate to the tastes of the group. Inexperienced food-planners may need tips on simple nutritious dishes. (See Appendix 18.)
2. Determine a budget. Estimate a maximum dollar amount based on the size of the group, the number of meals, and the group's need for frugality. As a starting figure you may want to estimate $1.75—$3 per person per day.
3. Determine the quantity of each food item needed. Inexperienced planners may need to consult more experienced cooks.
4. Study prices and estimate cost. Total cost should be within allocated budget.
5. Arrange for cooking and serving equipment. Depending on the facility, the group may need to bring its own equipment. Always check what is available in advance. Permission needs to be obtained if the group is planning to use a church kitchen or to borrow equipment. Inventory of borrowed items should be made to be checked off upon return.
6. Purchase food.* Plan for time to shop in the days just before departure. If traveling space is quite limited, some shopping can be done upon arrival. Perishables or specialties of the location are naturals to purchase at the location.

*For a lengthy retreat, Rev. Larry Dobson, of New Jersey, arranges in advance with a supermarket near the location, asking the grocer to pack up the daily orders for pickup each morning. He informs the grocer of the daily $ limit and asks him to throw in snack items within that budget. Grocers will usually be glad to bill the group at the end of their stay and will give lots of extras, even discounts.

7. Organize food by meal. Use boxes or bags to cluster the food items for each meal (except that needing refrigeration) and prepare a detailed instruction list of the menu and preparation steps.

Cost-Cutting Ideas

a. Find a grocer and a baker who are willing to give a discount (often 10% or more).

b. Purchase ("day-old") breads and treats from a bakery thrift shop.

c. Collect fresh fruits and vegetables donated from church members' gardens.

d. Have committee organize requests for donations from parents:
   —deserts or snacks
   —a whole birthday party if their teen is having a birthday anywhere near retreat date.

e. Bring snacks along for *purchase* by participants. One person should be delegated responsibility for the safekeeping and collecting of money. Having specific purchase times simplifies the accounting.

f. Publicize a list of food needs in advance and have a box in a public place ready for donations.

8. Estimate preparation time. Inexperience and the spreading out of responsibility can delay the meal. However, if reasonable estimates of the time required are made, if people follow through, and if "waitable" meals are planned, then the meals can fit smoothly into the needs of the program and hungry stomachs.

In the experience that we have had with groups doing their own cooking, the *pros* generally outweighed the *cons*. P E O P L E   H A D
FUN—a math lesson, high feelings, and too much salt in the oatmeal.

LEARNING—some essential food items were left at home; so did without. Discovered resourcefulness not always a taste-bud delight; but on future retreats fewer oversights.

JOY and PLEASURE at good food, a service rendered, and a team accomplishment!

LOW-COST MEALS FOR FAMILY RETREATS

On family retreats an efficient system is to have each family prepare its own meals except for one or two potluck suppers with all the families. This procedure feeds people for the same cost that food would be at home, but suggests a need for individual preparation sites (cabins, trailers, or campsites).

To utilize mealtime to enhance larger group unity, another model has worked well, providing a facility exists for large common meals prepared in one kitchen. Each family is asked to estimate what it would spend on food (realistically) if it stayed home. When these dollar figures are combined by the food-planning committee, this becomes the maximum budget. Next, the committee parcels out food assignments to each family which total close to the family's own dollar estimate. To reduce the amount of time spent in meal preparation during the retreat, people are assigned to prepare large pots of main dishes in advance, to be reheated at camp. The committee then supervises others who help cook on the retreat. This model has worked for groups of thirty people and could be used with larger groups.

Mealtime can be a CHORE or COMMUNION. Careful planning in advance of the retreat can help prevent technical distractions and can increase the beauty in the partaking of the Lord's provisions.

15. Registration

Preregistration is often necessary for estimates of numbers and can serve to encourage people to make commitments to go on the retreat.

Procedure for Preregistration Needs to Include:

1. Cut-off date for signing up (after which no one else may go).
2. Prepayment of a small amount by each registrant (helps to strengthen commitment to go).

Who does it? If more than one group is going, then a registrar for each group should be assigned with one overall coordinator. (See Appendix 16.) The registrar will need to work closely with the treasurer, if he/she is not functioning as both, to keep track of funds and records of payment.

Other Pointers:

1. Some time needs to be designated for collecting the balance of money from each participant.
2. To those who have registered, send instructions on timing, what to bring, etc. For youth, letters to parents are in order.
3. Distribute and collect medical release/health waivers. (See sample, Appendix 15.)

16. Promotion

Publicity for the retreat can serve several vital functions:

It can help generate enthusiasm and recruit participants and potential leaders.

It can inform others in the church body of the purposes and activity of some of their members.

It can inform the larger community (other churches and the neighborhood folks) of what exciting things this group is about.

ACTION STEPS

The group needs to decide *who* is the target population for their advertising campaign. If no recruits are needed and the retreat planned is quite similar to previous ones the church has experienced, then minimal publicity is needed. In contrast, if the retreat is going to have an unusual format or program or is going to a unique place, others may want to know about it and the group may want to recruit new members.

Next, consider *where* to place promotional material. Newsletters and Sunday bulletin announcements tend to be read primarily by senior citizens and church-oriented adults. Flyers or posters around the church reach the people who come to church perhaps only at night or during the week. Letters can be sent to people who are on church lists but who do not frequent the building. Some frugal recruiters have combined the invitations with registration cards already stamped and addressed for the ease of new people to make a commitment to go. One letter can serve to invite, clarify the basic facts and goals, and inform what to bring. Remember to submit articles to the local newspaper or to other churches' bulletins and newsletters if recruitment is desired from a broader base.

Thought should be given to what *content* to include in the promotional materials. People will want to know the basic facts: dates, location, departure and arrival times and places, cost, purpose, who can go, and how to register. A shorter blurb can name the retreat and then state who to contact to find out the details. Other facts which will serve as lures can be included, such as special events planned, special resource people coming, group reduced rates, unique facilities, and hints at what to bring. Some groups have used the mystery element to attract participants, displaying a symbol or word all around the church and then inviting people to find out what it is all about.

The *form* of the publicity can make a great deal of difference. Neatness and visual attractiveness are helpful. The use of actual photographs can transmit some of the spirit. These can be used on posters or passed around at group gatherings. Artistic designs, cartoons, and humor tend to attract attention to the ad. (See Appendix 12.) The simplicity and largeness of the sign increase its impact (as all billboard advertisers know).

PEOPLE ARE THE BEST ADVERTISERS

A personal invitation goes a lot further toward persuasion than a piece of paper. Those who have been on prior similar retreats who have had a good experience can help transmit the spirit on a one-to-one level or in groups. Folks who have been in on the planning for the retreat make good promoters, too. They know the facts, are excited in spirit, and provide an example of commitment: "I'm going; why don't you join me?" Some churches have successfully given a series of parties for potential retreat and conference goers. During the party, pictures and slides, relevant games, personal testimony, good refreshments, and fun all helped to interest people in the coming events.

Retreats can even be used to advertise for other retreats. Skip Wilson, of the First Presbyterian Church in Rumson, New Jersey, while doing fieldwork in Kentucky, led a worship service through a phone call connected to his home church's P.A. system. Such a phone call could be set up as a conference call between people in a Sunday school class and people on the retreat.

Another long-range means of promotion was developed by Rev. Gary Jenkins, of West Hills Christian Church in Coraopolis, Pennsylvania. He made a filmstrip entitled *What Is a Retreat?* to introduce people to the value and dimensions of retreating. (Available for purchase at $5.)

Articles written after the retreat for church and local newspapers can have an impact.

Does all this talk of advertising and promotion sound too secular? Good promotion shows respect for God's people in three important ways:

It can be quite effective in tying the retreat group in with the larger church body.

It is a significant element in rumor prevention, replacing mystery with facts.

It can serve as a form of evangelism reaching out to those who do not already know what is in store for them on a Christian retreat.

GOD BECAME FLESH in order to communicate with persons. Thinking about the "who, where, what, and how" of more effective communication sharpens our evangelical skills.

17. Rumors

Are rumors relevant to retreating? YES. A few years ago, a rumor nearly killed the possibility of our church youth going on retreats in the future. This subject needs serious consideration while planning the retreat, in the leaders' awareness of what is going on during the retreat, and in looking at ways in which problems are handled.

EXAMPLE OF RUMOR-POWER

A group of new juniors highs, senior highs, and college students were on a joint retreat. One of the youngest girls saw some older fellows smoking on one of the trails. This young girl told several other retreaters that the boys were smoking marijuana.

The rumor went around for several hours before someone told a counselor. The counselor went to the director. The rumor was traced back to its source. The boys were identified by the girl. In talking with the fellows, there was no indication that they had been smoking "grass." They did admit to smoking cigarettes and acknowledged that they were in the wrong for breaking that rule of the camp. Based on past acquaintance with the boys and their present attitude, there was no reason to disbelieve them. Appropriate consequences were determined. The girl was informed of the action.

Two weeks after the retreat, the pastor got a call from an irate parent about how degenerate our church was for allowing the use of drugs on weekend retreats. The pastor listened, asked for the source of information and any details. He then called in the assistant pastor who had directed the retreat. Fortunately, a close trusting relationship existed between them. Another call confirmed that the rumor source was the parent of the young junior high girl.

Action was taken: The parent was called in and the situation was explained to her. She was satisfied by the new information about how the smoking of *cigarettes* had been handled. She agreed to call those to whom she had spread the rumor. The pastors contacted directly the concerned person who had called the church. Retreating was out from under!

HANDLING RUMORS

You cannot ignore a rumor or run from it if you expect to be able to function in the future.

Rumors may happen, and they need to be faced squarely. The situation is even more critical if the church has never had a retreat before and some are skeptical of its value or workability.

Things do go on during the retreat that leaders do not know about. They are not on the retreat to be 24-hour-a-day investigators or police.

Lynn Nelson

A RUMOR MAY BE TRUE. Do not assume anything at the outset.

When a rumor comes to you:

1. LISTEN. Get all the information you can and the names of any people potentially involved; find out what the situation was; what actually happened.

2. THANK the person for trusting you enough to tell you.

3. GO to the people named to fact-find further about attitude and action. You might say, "Here is what I heard. You are the only ones who can clarify the situation. What actually happened?" If the people resist answering, push them; let them know the consequences to the whole group if the rumor is not handled. If they admit to responsibility, then decide on the appropriate corrective action. (See Chapter 23.) If no one takes responsibility for the occurrence, then the total group should be involved in the corrective action.

4. RETURN to your initial information source to inform them of the action being taken so that they know that the problem is neither being ignored nor encouraged.

5. INFORM the responsible church board of the rumor, the nature of the incident, and what is being done. The confidential nature of the information needs to be stressed. The board needs to understand why they are being informed—not to spread the rumor further, but to arm them with the facts that can quash the rumor if it is brought to them. Any board member who breaks confidentiality needs to be confronted.

In handling rumors, public announcements are rarely warranted. They usually only spread the fire and the possibilities for further misunderstandings. Deal with the people involved in the rumor-mill individually when possible. However, if 50 percent of the congregation knows about the situation before it is dealt with, then a public announcement may be in order. If this occurs, the leaders need to take a look at their relationship not only with the group with which they are working but also with the large church family.

RUMOR PREVENTION

The best rumor prevention is a good offense in two areas: adequate and trusted leaders and informed board members.

Leaders should really know their group well (new leaders should at least be open to the group). If a young person feels that he or she will be attacked for sharing some problematic information, he or she will be less likely to volunteer it. If he or she trusts the leaders not to reveal sources and to deal fairly with a situation, he or she will more readily come and tell because he or she may not know how to handle the information alone.

Problem incidents may indicate the need for a higher leader/participant ratio. If the problem is not the need for more adult presence and supervision, it may be a lack of responsibility or involvement by the group participants.

Leaders need to be informed about and feel comfortable in dealing with the popular testing areas of drug abuse and sex questions. These problems get a lot of national publicity but may not be the major ones for your youth group. You may need to be more aware of areas like cliques, backbiting, or prejudice.

Board members and the church need to be informed. Mysteries breed fantasies. Spend time in discussing ground rules and procedures for handling problems with parents and board members. Once a group has established a track record for integrity and people know more of what to expect, rumors do not start or spread so easily. Encourage parents and boards to give the group and leaders feedback. As mutual trust grows, people on all sides will tend to take incoming reports of problems with a grain of salt until they have had time to check them out with the responsible party.

An element of building this respect is the action to inform the church about the goals and significant activities of the retreat. Too often people only hear generalizations about the "fun" experienced. The deeper reflective and commitment changes may not be evident for a time.

Set the precedent of reporting to the appropriate board a summary evaluation of each retreat, including both positives and negatives. Such honest evaluation will gain respect.

With exciting enough programs and information sharing going on, the power of rumors pales.

18. Budget

Retreats do not have to be expensive. What a retreat costs depends primarily on the group's choice of facilities, cooking, and transportation.

The most frequent categories for budget items are: lodging, food, transportation/insurance; program expenses—leaders, resources, films; scholarships; miscellaneous—grab-bag items, crafts.

Budgeting for the retreat need not be complicated. One way is to start by listing the known fixed expenses—room rates per person or the cost of a package deal for the weekend, travel expenses, and food cost.

Over the past few years, the fixed price for many package deals at camps and conferences which included food and lodging has ranged from $14 to $55 per person for a Friday to Sunday noon length of stay. (Program expenses and travel are not included.) Variations in price may occur because of the inclusion of evening snacks, meal quality, and the relative plushness of the facilities.

Total costs can be as low as $7.50 to $12.50 per person for the same length of stay if the group does its own cooking. This figure can include facilities, program expenses, and travel costs as well as food.

For tips on finding economical *lodging* and having low cost *meals,* see chapters 13 and 14. As a general rule, you can eat on a retreat at least as cheaply as at home.

TRANSPORTATION COSTS

Total retreat costs can be reduced by asking members of the congregation to "drive a car to camp." If they do not have a car or if they cannot drive that weekend, they are encouraged to give at least $10 to "send their car in absentia." Any contributions over the need could be put aside for future transportation.

Traveling trips can also be done reasonably. The "Get Out of Texas" trip to St. Louis, Chicago, and the Ozarks in rented VW vans cost $75 per person with $40 of that for transportation (Appendix 35). Arlo Reichter takes youth from First Baptist Church, Los Angeles, on overnight trips ranging from $3 to $7.50 per person. This figure does not include meals which are eaten out, but it does include entrance fees to special attractions and group rates at motels. A trip by the youth of Hatboro Baptist from Philadelphia to Maine cost a total of $15 per person (23 people) for four days and three nights (1970). The group stayed in the summer cabin of the group's advisers.

PROGRAM EXPENSES

With outside leaders coming in to help, the cost of the retreat will go up. Many resource people are willing to come for honorariums plus expenses. With forty people on a retreat, each one giving $2 toward the guest, an honorarium of $80 could be given. (An agreement on the amount should be made beforehand.) Remember that in the business world, people pay their resource people from $200 to $600 a day. Let's be sure to appreciate our guests who are willing to come for a token fee.

Program resources are another budget item. See the "Grab-Bag Resource Kit" in Chapter 9 for suggested items. The cost will depend on the number of people going and the amount of supplies already on hand that you can tap. Make up a list of items needed and let your congregation know; donations will come. If your group is not actually spending much now on program resources, start budgeting about $20 per retreat and slowly build a basic library of resources. If your church purchases church school supplies in bulk, try to work out permission to use those supplies for retreat programming and/or work out orders together.

SCHOLARSHIPS

We feel that no one should be excluded from a retreat due to lack of money. Some groups reduce the cost for such people by a fixed percentage or amount; others pay their entire way. We prefer asking the persons to invest some amount of cash in the experience, as a mark of the retreat's importance to them. Usually scholarship assistance is kept confidential. Sometimes monies raised by the group are used to reduce the cost for everyone. However, this may not adequately help the person who is hard up for cash. Be sensitive.

Leaders who go on retreats should not be charged. They are investing their time, skills, and energy, and perhaps their cars. Figure the amount of leaders' expenses into the cost of the weekend to be divided among participants. Some leaders may want to pay. Fine! But give them the option of being the group's guests.

WHAT TO DO WHEN YOU'VE OVERSPENT

1. The bill may be quickly paid (personally or out of the church budget), or depending on the circumstances, the bill may be left temporarily unpaid to increase pressure on the group for assuming responsibility.
2. Determine the WHY of the cost overrun. Did something cost more than anticipated? Why didn't we know its cost? Was the estimate off or was the estimate ignored? What can we do to prevent this problem in the future?
3. Decide on corrective action to meet the obligation. Discuss what the group feels would be the best way to get the money to pay (or pay back) the bill. It may be easiest to charge each person on the retreat an additional amount, or the group may want to schedule a special fund-raising event to meet the deficit.
4. Be sure to include the "overspent" reasons in the retreat evaluation/summary so that the lessons learned will not be lost to groups in the future.

BUDGETING FOR RETREATS

We hope that church boards will consider a regular budget item for retreats. Retreats can be a powerful way for a board to move toward some of its goals. If your board or committee submits a proposed budget once a year, include at least $100 as seed money for retreating.

The general church budget may include money for a yearly church planning retreat. A number of churches are doing this. Amounts budgeted vary from $25 to $500, depending on the type of retreat envisioned, its length, and focus.

In churches where money is not budgeted for retreats, try this approach. Put an item in the proposed budget for a one-year trial basis for a church planning retreat. Show how the money will be spent. Plan carefully. Have a good event. Evaluate and report. People will be surprised at how much was accomplished and hopefully will be "sold" on including a larger amount for retreats another year.

19. Fund Raising

Churches vary (even within denominations) in their attitudes about fund raising as part of the regular church program. Some churches do not allow ANY fund-raising events. They may be overreacting to the seeming money focus of churches which are continually having bazaars, sales, and the like.

Fund raising can become an end in itself. If and when it does, it should be discontinued. Youth groups with poorly defined goals may fall into the trap of doing one fund-raising project after another and amassing a large treasury, because it provides easily measured results and gives the illusion of group movement.

Even in a church with a concept of tithing rather than buying, there may be permission for *some* fund raising for youth. The rationale for this permission is that younger junior highs do not usually have access to cash except from their parents and also that many youth appreciate more what they have worked for rather than having to be dependent on a giver and gift. The responsible board may be willing to define and agree upon specific purposes and types of projects which are permissible, so that it is not necessary for the youth to bother the board for each particular event.

POSSIBLE PROJECTS

SALES: notepaper, light bulbs, gift items, cards, rummage; food—candy, cakes, hoagies; pancake suppers, breakfasts, banquets, strawberry festivals.

SERVICES: "slave days"; help-a-homeowner day; work at church and "earn" $1.50 per hr. for youth budget; bike or hike with dollar commitments per mile; family film nights; Halloween insurance; car washes.

Some of the factors to be considered in deciding upon a fund-raising project are these:

1. Youth are willing to work hard for short periods of time, but it is much harder for them to sustain their enthusiasm over a period of months.
2. Many groups in the community also sell things.
3. The sale of items usually means that money has to be invested in inventory, sales accounted for, and goods distributed.

4. Perishable inventories of food carry the risk of spoilage and overpurchasings. Such items are usually best handled by advance orders or sales.
5. Decisions about techniques have to be related to the amount of money needed and the time available for a project.

In the light of these factors, projects which provide SERVICES to individuals or groups seem to be best.

The quickest, most easily organized project seems to be a car wash. Groups can raise $60 to $90 on one Saturday with only eight to ten people working ($1.75 donation per car). With a larger, well-organized group working in cooperation with a gas station, it is possible to make over $300 in one day. Church parking lots and car-wash (self-operated) lots are popular locations.

Doing a good job will often bring extra donations and return customers. One adult should be present to help handle any problems. We have found it best not to let the youth drive the cars, although in some cases they are quite responsible. (Part of the fun with car washes are the water fights. However, the fun should not interfere with the quality and timing of the service. Each group will have to find its own balance in this respect.)

Bake sales can be held simultaneously with the car wash. Reasonable prices usually result in sellouts. Most shopping centers will allow bake sales. You will want to check with the management to arrange a schedule and location.

Another project which netted our groups good money for the proportion of effort was the sale of Halloween Cleanup Insurance.

About three weeks before Halloween the group began to ask for donations for the cleanup policy. For a $2 donation per house, the group guaranteed that they would clean up any Halloween messes of the usual nature—pumpkins, tomatoes, waxed windows, etc. The group did not agree to repair any major damage, such as broken windows or spray paint.

Most years very few houses needed the cleaning. We checked with all the policyholders by phone the day after Halloween and then went around to clean up. If no cleanup was needed, we thanked them for their support.

One year the group netted over $80 and ended up cleaning only four houses and one car—three hours' work. It could be that in your area, damage is extensive and the group might be cleaning windows for days. Even so, at $2 a house, it's fun and a service.

FUNDING LONG TRIPS

If a group is raising money for a big trip, the approach for raising money has to be more long range in focus and worked out in more detail. If you need $2,000 two years from now, that means $1,000 a year. If you did one project each two months, you would need to average about $170 each event. If you planned a sales program, you would need to figure carefully the volume of sales needed to clear your profit. Consider also the number of man-hours which are available and the dollar yield anticipated per man-hour.

The members of one group spent several months developing a musical/drama program for fund raising for a missions service trip. They offered their program to other churches in the area in exchange for a freewill offering or a guarantee of $40 minimum, whichever was higher. People gave more generously when the purpose of the fund raising was shared.

(Not all fund raising has to occur before the trip— members of such a prepared group as mentioned above could sing for their supper and lodging along the way. The itinerary and arrangements need to be made ahead of time.)

CONTRIBUTIONS

Another area which is often overlooked is approaching individuals in the congregation for special contributions for specific projects. This is appropriate primarily when a major project is envisioned, and it should not be done without the knowledge of the group responsible for raising the church budget. Individuals with means are often happy to be approached for a contribution for a worthwhile project.

It is best to have an articulate member of the group make the presentation (with an adult leader if it is for a youth group). Set up an appointment in advance and make clear the purpose; perhaps say, "We would like to talk with you about our group's special project for. . . ."

Be prepared for your presentation. (You might want to role-play the presentation in advance, anticipating possible questions.) Describe the goals of the group and how the group is going about accomplishing them. Show how you have broken down the financial need and explain that the group itself is putting a great deal of direct energy into raising money. Show also what amount of money you are trying to raise through contributions. Theories vary on whether one should ask for a specific amount. If you decide in advance what you are asking for, you can honor the person as well as challenge him. Some prefer an open-ended question, such as: "How much do you feel you could give?" or "Would you be willing to help us in reaching our goal? How much then would you be willing to give?"

If the group has slides or pictures related to the proposed project, the presentation is enhanced.

One or two good contributions can save thousands of hours of work and can free the group to focus on activities other than raising money.

PROBLEMS IN DISTRIBUTION

In one group with which we worked, differences developed about how the money raised by the group was to be used. Some of the people who had worked HARD did not want the money to go into a common pot to reduce the cost of the retreat for everyone—including those who stayed home or goofed off. If this problem arises, you have an excellent opportunity for (1) practicing conflict resolution, and (2) discussing a number of very real feelings and values.

We learned that it is helpful to clarify *before* the fund-raising project itself how the money will be distributed and used. Then people are more conscious about what will be the consequences of their contribution.

Fund raising can become an end in itself OR it can be an opportunity for

        SERVICE,   personal investment,
             team building,
                extending personal skills,
     sharing the spirit of LOVE.

20. Insurance

The subject of insurance needs to be approached from several angles before setting out on a retreat. Is the group covered by the regular policy of the congregation? What coverage is already there? Usually there is liability, but the medical/accident limitations are not adequate. Explore the matter with the board of trustees or some other official body to determine the present coverage.

The church has the option of securing additional insurance to cover group trips throughout the whole year. A number of companies have policies of this sort designed to cover Scout troups or youth groups. We were able to obtain a policy for $1 per person for a year from the agent who handled the rest of the church insurance. You will want to check with your church's insurance agent.

Other options are available. Some groups purchase insurance for each trip (10 to 15 cents per person per trip). We felt it easiest to handle things once and for all for the whole year.

Money to cover the policy can come out of the church budget, the youth budget, or out of the registration for each event. Sometimes camps include insurance in the cost of their package deals. Check to see if this is the case.

See what it covers, whether it is a duplication of the insurance which the group already has, and whether the group is covered en route or only upon arrival.

If rented vehicles are being used for transportation, the coverage provided by the rental agency needs to be clarified. Is additional coverage needed?

Individual drivers should also be asked to make sure that they have good auto insurance policies. This check is critical especially when younger drivers are involved, who may not be covered under a standard policy.

All this talk about insurance may sound paranoid. A group should not become insurance poor and there does not need to be excessive coverage. However, thought should be given to this area to be sure that in case of difficulties, the group or the church or the individual driver would not be placed in an awkward legal or financial position. In planning for a trip, the church has an obligation to "care for the sheep."

Check with your agent. Raise the question of what constitutes adequate coverage with the advisory body of the congregation. They can and should help make such determinations.

21. Transportation

Why travel? To get AWAY from the everyday familiars!

Traveling to the retreat location is an integral part of the retreat. Traveling may serve to expand the sense of community, broaden the base of experience, and increase the range of skills. When travel starts, the retreat has begun! It is important to think about how the travel is to be accomplished.

HOW TRAVEL?

Possible vehicles are:
9-passenger station wagons or
  12-15-passenger vans.
These are IDEAL
  for allowing group spirit
  to develop en route!
Even larger BUSES are fun!

Most of us have to settle for a regular sedan which does not allow as much room for subgroups to intermingle as do vans or buses.

For longer trips some groups use rented vehicles to obtain the kind of transportation they want. This rental increases the cost of the trip per person, but it is still a very reasonable option, even in an emergency shortage of vehicles for a short trip. Care must be taken to be sure that the insurance coverage by the company or church is adequate for the intended use. It is better to pay for extra coverage if the standard coverage is not deemed adequate.

Most of the time, people who know each other want to travel together. If using cars, we usually try to allow for both comfort and challenge by asking several from different friendship groups to ride together. New friendships may emerge through this trip together.

CARAVANS?

On trips we have generally found that it is better for cars not to try to travel together. Attempting to stay together can lead to a number of driving hazards:

1. The cars in back are constantly trying to watch the cars in front and not the road.

2. The people in the cars may be waving and shouting to each other between cars which can be distracting to the drivers.
3. There is a fear of getting separated if drivers do not independently have directions; hence drivers might cut safety corners (such as run yellow lights) in order to keep up.

ROAD RALLIES

We prefer to make longer trips somewhat like a road rally, not for saving time but for precision. Each car tries to arrive at the destination and points along the way within an estimated time limit. Time-limit estimates should be made with road conditions and speed limits in mind. Drivers are informed of the goal for average speed. Rest-stop time needs to be included.

Instruct drivers who discover that they are going to be more than an hour (or other time determined by group) late to call the retreat facility so that others who arrive ahead will not worry.

Each car has a treasurer who is given a predetermined amount of money to cover tolls and gasoline for the trip. He/she is to keep a record of all expenses. Another person may be asked to be a copilot to keep track of the premarked map and route instructions. Someone may want to keep track of time and mileage information. See

Appendix 17 for a sample form. Many get to learn a new skill. Using this rally technique, we had six cars of youth traverse seven states with no one getting lost except for one initial false start.

STOPPING

We usually allow each carload to decide whether to stop for snacks on trips up to three hours in length. Groups of youth usually want to stop. Sometimes we will all agree to meet at a certain place if we know the route. Each car gets there in its own time with no attempt to race.

LOST?

It is good to meet with the drivers before departure to check into procedures. Discussing what to do if lost helps by anticipating a frustrating or possibly panic-producing occurrence in a safe setting. Frank handling may reduce embarrassment or anxiety. Tips can be shared about how to get back on a limited access road if you took the wrong turn or how to find out where you are and get back to the route by asking questions at gas stations, restaurants, or of police.

WHO DRIVES?

On youth trips it is important to establish beforehand who is designated as the driver and codriver. As a general rule, we tried to avoid having youth under twenty-one drive at all. However, there were times when we could not get enough older adults to drive and had to use responsible youth. When this occurred, we made sure that there was an adult present to help with any problem and to discourage any tendency for driving horseplay.

Listen to the reactions of the youth to their trip, and you can learn a lot about how they felt about the quality of their drivers. Many are at the point of learning to drive themselves, and they are watching closely how others drive. Even if they are overcritical, you can soon learn who not to ask again.

When we used a youthful driver, we secured written permission from the parents of those riding in his car that it was OK for their son/daughter to ride with that person driving. We also checked with the parents of the *driver* to make sure that his/her driving was responsible and OK with them and to review their insurance coverage for adequacy in case of accident or injury.

The "Get Out of Texas" group had each registering youth have his/her parents sign a legal waiver for health and a permission note for their youth to drive the van in case of disability of the regular driver. This is an excellent idea for retreats that entail much driving.

In summary, each driver needs:

1. A marked map and/or written route directions (even if they have driven there before).
2. Name and address of destination.
   Name of person in charge to call in case of emergency.
   Phone number of destination.
   Procedure for phone charge: collect? charge to church phone? charge to home phone?
3. Name of contact person at home and phone number.
4. Insurance information on car and group.
   Car registration information.
   Driver's license, of course!

OPTIONAL

5. Car treasurer, money, logbook

AND

A VEHICLE IN GOOD RUNNING ORDER!

WE ARE HERE!

22. *Organizational and Environmental Strategies*

WHAT TO DO UPON ARRIVAL

Arrival basically involves knowing where to go and what to do thereafter. If the group is traveling separately, then each car must know where to go. Is the group to wait for everyone before doing anything? Or have decisions been made earlier so that the first groups to arrive can begin moving things in and preparing the facility for the rest of the group?

Have the cabin or sleeping assignments been predetermined or are they to be decided after the group arrives? If program areas have been designated, resource materials can be unloaded.

Time needs to be allowed for unpacking and for individual exploration of the new environment.

It is critical that group members meet together soon after arrival to set the tone for their time together. This gives everyone a chance to review PURPOSES and GROUND RULES for the group and facility, to sign up for K.P. and other maintenance or program groups, and to have some celebration—refreshments or singing. Many times groups will also structure "getting to know you" activities or will begin the weekend's program. (See Program Ideas Chart for openers.)

DIVISION OF LABOR

The division of labor can be handled all at once rather than taking time for it on each occasion when needed. Anticipating the maintenance needs and signing people

75

up for them in the initial session is an efficient method.

If the group is going to be broken up into smaller groups for program activities, divisions may be made ahead of time, or after arrival. Such groupings can be done by *chance* (for example, by distributing puzzle pieces or candy-colored tongue depressors), by *choice,* or by *assignment.*

MAKING THE PLACE OURS

There needs to be a balance between "making the place ours" and respecting the beauty, natural setting, and the other people sharing the facility. The group needs to feel at home, and the process of getting to feel at home can be a task that unifies the group. For example, posters can be made during leisure time to be hung up around the dining area. "We created this, it is ours." (Displaying individuals' work also helps them feel appreciated and involved.) Other craft creations can be used in building an environment uniquely "ours."

Some groups have hung large sheets of butcher paper or table-covering paper on the walls as GRAFFITI boards for group creativity. We have had great responses to open-ended statements, such as: "love is . . .; I wish . . .; I hate . . .; I get angry at . . .; I love . . .; guys are . . .; girls are . . .; people are. . . ." You can think up more. (Magic markers on long strings are great; check to be sure ink will not go through to the wall.)

In addition to graffiti boards, many groups have used MESSAGE boards to keep people posted on the schedule and any changes.

Music can also be used for ownership. Decisions about its use need to be made in light of the program goals. We have sometimes requested youth to bring a favorite record album. These were then played at one or two meals a day—low volume to encourage conversation. (If there are other groups eating in the same area as you, the feelings of different generational groups may need to be considered.) Some specific songs/selections were also used in discussions, Bible study, and worship.

RELATIONSHIP TO OTHERS USING THE FACILITIES

It is helpful to find out in advance which other groups will be sharing the facilities with you. You then have the opportunity of corresponding with that group to find out age, numbers, purpose of the weekend, and related information. You can then plan program or worship items together as appropriate. Schedule conflicts can also be anticipated and possibly worked out.

The leader, at least, should meet the other program directors and head counselors who are sharing the facility while you are there. Know WHO is in CHARGE and be able to recognize them if problems develop. It is also helpful to know the other group's rules and to have them understand yours.

If you have not met the director of the retreat facility itself, take time to seek him/her out for mutual exchange of information: ground rules (his/hers/yours), goals, schedules, who's who, and the like. These precautions will contribute to smooth relationships.

23. *Handling Problems*

The best way to handle problems during the retreat is to do everything you can to PREVENT them from happening before the event. Well-trained leaders and careful planning of the program, schedule, and location—all geared to fit the needs and goals of the group—are the best preventive medicine. A prayer a day will not keep the troubles away if you have not done good planning and allowed the Holy Spirit to guide you.

Planning will reduce problems but not eliminate them. If you anticipate a way of handling them and realize their potential for helping you, the group, and the individuals in it to GROW, problems will be a less destructive hassle.

"That kid/adult will never change. I'm powerless."
versus
"Everything is possible for anyone who has faith" (Mark 9:24).

"The factions will never get together."
versus
Jesus chose the most implausible array of warring factions to be his disciples; they became brothers in him.

The desired attitude is to recognize each problem as a potential "teachable moment" which can transform the life of the person and the group. None of us is perfect, we all err; we are sinners forgiven and saved by grace. Let us be a part of building a caring community in which mistakes can lead to growth/improvement and can be a vehicle through which God's redemption comes.

STRATEGY

WHO will handle the problems and HOW they will be handled need to be made clear to the group from the outset. (See chapter 12 on Ground Rules for the process for doing this.)

The discussion of rules and consequences needs to be geared to the emotional maturity of the people involved. Discussing consequences of violations not even being considered by people in the group is a waste of energy and it breeds mistrust. There are some advantages to waiting until an issue actually arises before determining what the consequences will be. In this way, the consequence can be tailored to fit the individual situation. Also, the danger that discussion of potential issues will lead to their occurrence is avoided.

Prevent escalation. Problems won't disappear by ignoring them. Detecting and dealing with problems immediately helps prevent escalation. Factors which help make early detection a reality are:
- mutual trust between group and leaders,
- good counselors,
- attitude of openness/honesty in group,
- attitude of confident expectation on the part of leaders that every problem, with the help of God, can be handled and resolved.

© 1975 King Features Syndicate

If the leader or rules-enforcement group is not at ease in its own position, then the situation can escalate more easily into a power play or win-or-lose situation.

Some small problems may loom large due to low tolerance for dealing with problems. Tolerances may be lowered because there are too few staff, or they are overworked, tired, and edgy. Minor issues may also develop into a major battle because the complainer may have a "hidden" major complaint that he/she is not sharing. Try to smoke out the larger underlying issue by asking open-ended questions, such as, "Is there something else about the retreat which is bothering you?" "Are your feelings and actions based only upon this single occurrence?"

Distinguish between fact and rumor.

TACTICS

What to do when problems arise:

1. MEET with those people involved or accused of having been involved. Clarify what actually happened—gathering all versions and trying to discover the most accurate account. Whom do you believe, and why? If you do not feel that anyone is being honest, state that. Then begin working out a strategy for the whole group involved in the offense—treating them all equally.

2. PRAY as leaders, and pray with those involved in a major incident. Warning: prayer is NOT preaching or moralizing. Prayer is listening and talking with God. Have some time of complete silence for tuning in.

Moralizing: "God, help this kid to see how bad he has been. . . ."

Sharing: "God, I am discouraged. I feel like. . . . Help us to know what is best for us to do. . . ."

If the tone of sharing has been set by the leader in prayer, the offender may be more willing also to share honestly.

3. Gauge the DEGREE OF SEVERITY of the offense. Any consequences should be fair; the degree of correction should be consistent with the degree of offense.

The following listings of effects will help in seeing their severity in perspective. The most serious effects are listed first, moving down to matters of lesser consequence.

Effects on Individuals:

1. endangers life (overdose, drunken driving, etc.)
2. increases possibility of legal action
3. induces potential addiction
4. causes potentially deep emotional hurt (rejection, depression, guilt, unwanted pregnancy, disease, loss of self-esteem)
5. limits or narrows life choices

6. risks condemnation by respected authorities
7. loses respect from others

Effects on Immediate Group:

1. endangers the physical lives of others in the group
2. causes emotional impact on others in group (many hurt deeply)
3. risks the continued existence of the group
4. hurts things or people
5. necessitates repair or amending
6. risks reputation of the group
7. interrupts program

Effects Beyond Immediate Group:

1. endangers lives of people outside of group
2. hurts own family, other families; possible loss of job for church staff
3. damages property of others, delaying or eliminating use by others
4. damages reputation of church or facility
5. risks the existence of program for others in future

4. Discover the ATTITUDE OF THE OFFENDERS toward the group and leaders, and observe their actions.

Possible Intentions:

1. purposeful—with malice
   —with indifference
   —for fun, not thinking
2. rebellion: "Let's see who is the boss around here. I dare you. . . ."
3. unthinking action escalation: "We just got carried away."
4. not recognizing the wrong: actions based on subculture value system which gives the OK; or emotionally ill.
5. unaware of rules—didn't pay attention
   —rules not determined
   —rules not publicized
   —rules vague.

It is important to separate the doer from the offense. Your standards in judging others will be used to judge you. (See Mark 4:24.) What goes into a man is not what makes him unclean. It is what comes out of the man which is evidence of his evil intentions and wrong spirit. (See Mark 7:14-23.) You have heard it said, "An eye for an eye . . ." but I say, "Love your enemies . . . do good to those that hate you, and pray for them who use or persecute you." You are to be the children of your Father . . . for he maketh his sun to rise on the evil and on the good, and sendeth rain on the just and on the unjust. (See Matthew 5:38-48.)

5. Examine the LEADER'S ATTITUDE toward the misbehavior. There may be a problem with double messages: the leader may anticipate the mischief with secret glee, but be judgmental at the same time. Double messages are very confusing; when this is happening, the leader needs to be confronted (see p. 81).

6. CLARIFY various alternative consequences or corrective actions and consider the potential impact of these upon the individuals and the broader group. (If potential consequences will seem unduly strong to the larger group, enforcing them may increase rebellion.)

Possible corrective actions by offenders:
(demonstrations of caring)

1. Perform service to those hurt.
2. Repair broken or damaged items.
3. Give money for replacement of damage, or work a certain number of hours at a mutually agreed upon dollar per hour value.
4. Perform symbolic acts of penitence (determined by the group).
5. Allow "one-mistake" policy—a person has one chance to make a mistake without corrective action, but not a second one of the same kind. (If this policy exists, it might best be unadvertised. It would also be inappropriate for a large "unknown group" where such action might be taken to mean, "you don't really mean what you say; therefore, there must be no limits.")

Look at the choice of corrective action in terms of consistency with past actions for similar offenses. The situation may warrant individual handling, but take care not to grant special privileges.

Look also at the timing involved. Is it the first day of the event, or the last? How can the retreat setting and the group be used in the consequences?

7. CHOOSE APPROPRIATE ACTION. The ethic involved is the new commandment: "That you love one another; even as I have loved you, that you also love one another" (John 13:34, RSV).

Example:

When a group of ninth and tenth grade boys had raided another group and done some damage to cabins and the grounds, the facility director came to the program director at breakfast and said that those involved in the raid were going to be sent home. He was going to call their parents himself.

The retreat leaders felt that his proposed solution was unfair. They did not justify the wrongdoing in any way, nor did they deny the distress caused to the other groups using the facility. However, had it been a raid at any other time, the consequences probably would not have been to be sent home.

At the leaders' insistence, the director agreed to meet with the offenders to clarify information, check out attitude, and then decide appropriate action. The after-breakfast meeting, which was promised the offenders when they were caught at 3:00 A.M., was held. The facility director's concerns were expressed: the other groups using the camp were already uptight due to other circumstances; so the raid caused extra fear and damage. The director himself was on edge because the facility was being evaluated that particular week.

The fellows raiding had not realized the magnitude of these factors, apologized, and expressed a willingness to set things right. When asked what they felt would be fair

EEK & MEEK   by Howie Schneider

Reprinted by permission of Newspaper Enterprise Association (or NEA).

recompense—evidence of their desire to be forgiven—they agreed to pay for damaged items, clean up any mess, and do some additional painting and fix-up of the facility.

The camp director felt their penitence was real, accepted their offer, and allowed the boys to stay. Had he held to his first hard-nosed stance, the retreat leaders would have met together with him to intercede for fair consequences.

8. DECIDE WHOM TO INFORM. When young people have broken ground rules, it is important to consider whether or not to inform parents. On minor and first offenses, such accounting to parents is usually not necessary, especially when the problem has been handled within the group. If breaking the rules becomes a pattern or if a major offense with far-reaching consequences occurs, it is only fair to inform parents, who have the ultimate responsibility. The leaders may feel that it is important to work with the parents as a team in handling continuing problems.

Rarely have we had to inform law enforcement agencies. Few illegal actions have occurred except for experimentation with drugs, and in most cases the leaders have felt that other options for corrective action are more effective than arrests.

Talking with the people who have violated the ground rules about the question of who should be informed helps offenders to take more seriously the effects of their actions.

9. See that the agreed-upon CORRECTIVE ACTIONS ARE CARRIED OUT.

10. LET THE REST OF THE GROUP KNOW how the immediate situation is being resolved and also if there are any changes in policy or definitions. The occurrence of a problem may be a good stimulus for a program session of discussion and/or role play.

11. FORGIVE AND FORGET. It is often very hard not to carry a grudge or not to expect the person to err again. "If your brother does something wrong, reprove him and, if he is sorry, forgive him . . ." (Luke 17:3-4).

Wrestling with a problem can be a time of discovering more about oneself and one's God. Witness Jacob and Saul. Let us trust more fully in God's redeeming power.

HANDLING SPECIFIC PROBLEMS

The rest of this chapter will give some examples of ways to handle specific problems in the following areas:
- who goes and who participates
- leaders shirking responsibilities
- participants not participating
- agenda pressure

- whose facilities
- angry ones and loners
- boundaries
- problems (primarily associated with youth)

1. eating	5. sex
2. sleeping	6. privacy
3. smoking	7. fighting
4. drugs	8. stealing

Who's Allowed?

When uninvited guests show up for the retreat, it may be a matter of poor communication about registration and transportation (see our Retreat Disaster, chapter 3), or a case of friendliness and curiosity on the part of people sharing the retreat facility.

Depending on the goals of the group, such invasion may not be a problem. In fact, in an evangelism, service, or even recreational retreat, others outside the group may be included by plan. However, when the group is focusing on a specific task of learning or is planning for its future or is working on group development, people from the outside who do not know the rules and goals may be a distraction. Lack of clarity about the retreat goals will make the decision harder.

Here are some *alternative actions* when the "invasion" is a problem:

1. Invite the visitors to stay if they agree to participate fully and abide by the ground rules.

2. Make clear the reasons that it is inappropriate for them to stay. Raise the possibility of joining together in the future.

3. Decide what activities planned most lend themselves to being shared and invite the visitors to participate in those, and explain the need for exclusiveness during other times.

4. If the outsiders are staff members of the retreat facility and they refuse to abide by the leaders' requests in regard to participation or distracting group members, then confront them and go with them to their supervisor if necessary.

5. If it appears that because visitors are present, the goals of the retreat are not being accomplished, you may want to open the problems before the group for discussion. Perhaps the group wishes to change its retreat goals.

6. If only a few of the group members are encouraging the distraction by visitors, then their lack of commitment to the retreat goals needs to be confronted. They may be given the option of increasing their level of commitment to the success of the retreat or leaving the retreat and going home.

Leaders Not Living Up to Responsibilities

Example One:

On a jointly planned two-week trip, one leader (A) was to have taken care of all the mechanical arrangements for the group: where to stay, menus, sleeping accommodations, and the like. The other leader (B) had taken this responsibility the previous year on their joint youth retreat. When the group arrived for the first night, there were not enough tents; so half the group slept in cars. As the trip progressed, Leader A would not take responsibility for enforcing any of the rules of the group among his youth. There was no cooperation on meal preparations and other duties.

Leader B was not willing to confront Leader A with his feelings and stuck it out for the whole trip, boiling inside. He realized later that this was not fair to himself, the other leader, or the group.

He might have blown up, decided that the trip was a farce, and ended it early. Another option which might have started resolution without ending the trip would have been for Leader B to say to Leader A, "I'm angry with you because I trusted you to do certain things which you said you would do (list), and you don't seem to be making any effort. What's happening? Are you willing to make a change?" If the discussion stimulated no willingness to change in Leader A, the retreat might best be cut short. However, the confrontation with honest feelings might have been what was needed to begin the change process.

Example Two:

One college-age youth, who had never experienced drugs, used the experimentation by individuals in the group as occasion for his own exploration. This clearly defeated his leadership function. He was trying to be a "cool guy" and also a "leader," sometimes reporting incidents and other times not. The group lost respect for him.

When leaders are not able to respond in an adult way to problems (they may send inconsistent messages, go into a rage, or completely ignore the problem), then other problems arise in addition to the original. Leaders who have difficulty handling or sharing their emotions may be dealt with in several ways:

1. The group may learn to respect them as human beings who have limits, admit their lack of perfection, and want to change;

2. The group may maintain acceptance and respect for them even if the leaders refuse to admit that they were in error;

3. The group may reject them because they appear to be indifferent to the grief their behavior is causing.

It is sometimes difficult for an adult who is in a leadership position to accept himself or herself as imperfect and to accept God's forgiveness and the forgiveness of the group for inappropriate behavior. Admission of error is difficult for most people of any age.

The leader may not feel that his or her behavior is a problem. Consequently he/she may not want to change. If the problem behavior occurs during the retreat, the group may probably choose to stick the weekend through and then later make a decision about whether this person should be invited as a leader on future retreats. However, the situation is more difficult if the individual is involved as a regular leader of the group. Then the board responsible for leadership of the group may have to ask the person to resign if he/she is unwilling to try to change. This action is very hard for a board to do. Nevertheless, setting limits and not encouraging destructive behavior is the LOVING thing to do.

"Participants" not Participating

Several elements in planning the retreat can help prevent this problem. If it has been made clear that those who register also agree to the program and ground rules, then those who do come will have made that commitment. If the planning has been done by quite a number of people on the retreat, then they have an investment in seeing it carried through.

We have experienced lack of involvement on retreats precisely when there is the feeling that *"they* decided it, not *I."*

The signs of dissatisfaction with the program will be obvious: people arriving late to groups, people not willing to talk, people raising questions other than those up for discussion, people skipping meetings or refusing to participate in activity, people sitting "quasi-attentive" but basically uninvolved.

This general dissatisfaction is harder to deal with than specific rebellion in doing certain tasks, such as meal preparation or cleanup. Specific contingencies can be placed on specific tasks, for example, "There will be no supper tonight unless five people sign up to prepare it."

In handling the larger dissatisfactions with the overall program, you may decide to ignore them and try to do better the next time. If large numbers of people are not participating, another option would be to bring the fact of the indifferent or hostile feelings out into the open for discussion and decision making about what can be done to improve the retreat or increase participation. If it is discovered that there are several factions with different interests, then other program options may be created— although this takes lots of energy and extra leadership. If the problem runs deep and involves many group members, and no immediate resolution is in sight, the group can decide to stick it through, or to admit the futility of the situation and return home early.

Evaluation is crucial! Getting feedback on quality of leadership, personal goals, decision-making styles, and group process will give the leaders more information to work with in planning the next moves of the group.

Note: If a board or committee is going on a planning retreat and families have been invited, clarification is needed as to who is expected to participate in the various sessions of the group. Sometimes the spouses and teens are welcome in the program sessions of the committee, sometimes not.

Agenda Pressure

If you are getting the feeling that you are behind schedule or that you are not getting enough accomplished, it is good to stand back and look and listen:

1. How are the rest of the staff feeling? How is the group feeling about timing?
2. Is what we are trying to cover realistic for the time we have and for this group?
3. Is too much happening or not enough? Is there a lack of meaning in the items being done?

Rather than being overwhelming, the agenda may be boring. When people are complaining about not having enough to do, check out your assumptions about your participants' ability to use nonstructured or lightly structured time. They may be unfamiliar with the activity options due to lack of exposure to them before, for example, when a city youth goes to the country, or vice versa. Have some quick alternative ideas and have a resource bag handy. Also look at the retreat goals. Perhaps the goals were not in fact defined and the group is sensing the lack of direction.

The pressure of having too much outlined to do is also real. Maybe the planning committee was overly optimistic about what could be accomplished and planned enough material for two retreats. Or, maybe someone had a hard time making choices and left everything in. If there are obviously going to be too many elements to accomplish, sit down for a few minutes as a leadership team to take an overview of where the group is, what the group has done, and what still is to be done. Which of the remaining elements/activities is most related to what you still want to accomplish? Which can be omitted? Time will omit them for you; so you have a choice: decision by default—let the clock do it—or decision by consciously choosing the most important elements.

BE OPEN TO REVISING SCHEDULED AC-TIVITIES. Don't let the ticking of the clock or the schedule on paper rule the day.

Whose Facilities? ("Move over, please")

Your program may be annoying to other people using the grounds or vice versa. Negotiations are always possible. Be aware that there may be people with different tastes and styles of retreating who are sharing the facility.

If your group is criticized about a program item, usually an acceptable compromise is possible: for example, hold the activity in another area, at another time, or perhaps modify it. If you take a stand to maintain your activity unaltered, you will need to weigh the risk of not being welcomed back, and you must accept the consequences produced by your actions.

It can help a great deal to let the director of the facilities (if there is one) know the orientation, goals, and philosophy of your group. He or she then can help interpret your program to others if they come to him/her with questions.

Know your facilities and their orientation and rules in advance. Go there expecting to work within their rules, even if they seem arbitrary or unfair. Otherwise, someone in the group needs to contact the director in advance and request specific exceptions or alternatives for your group. Such exceptions are sometimes made (see p. 84).

The relationship between the retreat group and the regular staff of the facility may be problematic, each expecting the other to conform to his or her needs and convenience. It takes give on both sides. When a problem occurs, it is best first to deal with the person one-to-one. Level with each other about feelings, reasons for timing or rules, options, etc. If there is no settlement, THEN go to the person's staff supervisor together with the staff person, and try to work out a common solution. The joint decision making will most likely prevent resentment on the staff person's part toward you and your group. Be sure your requests are reasonable in light of the facilities, available staff, group size, etc. (You may not be able to get the canteen to open at 2 A.M.!)

Be ready to propose alternatives and compromise solutions.

Aggressive Angry People and Quiet Withdrawn People

Within every group of adults or youth, there will usually be one or two very aggressive people and one or two who are quiet and withdrawn. The latter are not often considered "group problems," but they should be considered so, because their potential is not being realized by themselves or the group. Both the individual and the group are being cheated. The silent majority also has a problem if it allows itself to be dominated by the aggressive people and does not come up with a way of dealing with them.

Loud aggressive persons need to have their energies directed so they are a less disruptive force within the group. They can be specifically used in some leadership capacities. After they have "done their thing" and gotten positive feedback for it, they may be more willing to share the spotlight with someone else.

In group work, it is sometimes helpful to put all the aggressive persons in the same small group and the quiet ones in another. The loud ones can then fight it out among themselves and the others have more "air-time" in their group. Sometimes the divide-and-conquer strategy works better, especially if one person is "fed his lines" by a buddy. (If they are working as a team, use their talents, but structure them.) If the two are split up in different small groups, they just may emerge as different persons.

Special thought needs to be given to including the quiet individual in the group. Asking embarrassing or direct questions during a discussion or program is usually not the best way to proceed. Getting to know the person on a one-to-one basis—discovering interests, talents, and the like—is a good first step. Then help construct the

---

GOD can be present even in a water balloon fight!

We had a young seventh grade boy who was immature for his age socially, but was very bright. He was constantly being picked on by the older members of his group and by older guys in the senior high group. Of course he did plenty of things to encourage being picked on!

The counselor spent a good deal of time talking and praying about the whole situation. The boy was befriended by a counselor, and his interests were explored. An area was found in which he could contribute constructively in the program. He did his preparation well, and his contributions were accepted and appreciated by the group. His attitude toward the group began to change as well.

The actual SYMBOL of his acceptance by the group came when he was invited to participate in a water balloon fight with the older guys. It was a real "baptismal experience" for him—a new life, a new experience of God's love. He was never the same.

---

program to include items in which such a person may contribute his/her talent and receive appreciation from the group. *EVERYONE* has some talent or interest which can be capitalized upon. If we think they are hopeless, we just don't know them well enough, or we need to ask for "new eyes" in viewing them.

It is important to have enough leaders along so that some can be free to be with individuals on a one-to-one basis as needed. Aggressive people and loners are all asking for attention and acceptance.

Another way which some have found helpful for dealing with behavior problems is behavior modification, using the techniques of rewarding acceptable behavior and ignoring or giving negative feedback for destructive behavior.[1]

God is at work in every crisis. Opportunities for growth are always present. We need eyes to see, and faith to act.

Boundary Problems

"But I didn't know where the edge of camp was," says he, five miles toward town.

Boundary expectations for all retreats need to be clarified. If the participants are adults or family groups, are they expected to stay together during the experience, or is each family free to plan its own activities? What if some want to go bowling when something else has been planned? These kinds of decisions need to be made prior to the retreat event while selecting the goals for the retreat.

On youth retreats, time boundaries may be of concern as well as space boundaries—bedtime or leaving time. Youth tend to want to extend the time as long as possible. Definite limits need to be set. Clarify also, before the retreat and during orientation, the rule that no one is to leave the grounds without specific permission. (Usually a condition of granting permission to drive cars to the retreat is agreement by youthful drivers not to drive while there.)

Within the limits, be willing to consider wild suggestions—going out for sodas/pizza at 1:00 A.M. (requirements: open to all who are awake—no special privileges; find a counselor who is willing to go along); special late-night hikes (same requirements) as long as leaders are notified who is going—youth and leaders— departure time, expected time of return, and actual time of return.

[1] See *Respond, Volume 2* (Valley Forge: Judson Press, 1972), pp. 129-130.

Problems More Associated with Youth Retreats

1. Improper Eating

A young junior high boy brought a suitcase full of candy on a retreat and proceeded to eat it throughout most of one day. He did not eat anything at the meals. The message given him by his counselor was: "If you continue eating candy all day, you will be sick tomorrow. I do not want you to be sick; so I would like to see you stop eating candy and eat right."

He got sick and spent the next day in bed. He tried to use his illness as an attention-getting device. This was foiled by intentionally ignoring him except for a short visit during the morning and afternoon to establish contact—no extra attention. The counselor asked some reflective questions: "Do you know why you are sick? Who made you eat the candy? Is it a comfortable feeling today? What have you learned?"

The boy was up and ate a bit of dinner. He ate well the next day and never brought candy on a retreat again. Several other youth also learned from his experience. It was firsthand learning.

The behavior of this boy was self-regulating. He was allowed to experience the natural physiological consequences of his actions, and because they were unpleasant, he decided to change. Many behavioral situations can be handled this way, except that we as adults are not willing to put up with the sick, whiny kid when he makes mistakes.

This way of handling problems works best when the consequences are immediate as opposed to long range, such as problems related to drugs and sex.

2. Sleeping

Young people often do not want to go to bed. They are full of energy and excitement for living. The wise retreat planning committee will take this into account in its plans. (See options, p. 49.)

When there is a bedtime established, it is helpful to remember the need for transition periods. Shifting from a high level of activity to settling down does not happen with an announcement. Develop a warning system. It might include "lights out in fifteen minutes," "lights out in five minutes." Perhaps give an extra five minutes and then with firmness say, "OK, lights out." You can handle any hassle with confidence, for you have bent over backwards to be fair. Don't put up with additional procrastination techniques. Depending on your goals and rules, "lights out" may mean silence or quiet talking or just being in your sleeping area. Be sure everyone is clear on the intention.

IF GROUP MEMBERS ARE GIVEN THE OPTION OF STAYING UP LATER THAN THEY NORMALLY DO AT HOME, MAKE CLEAR THAT THEY ARE EXPECTED TO LIVE UP TO THE CONSEQUENCES OF THEIR DECISION. This means that they are NOT going to stay home from school "sick" on Monday because they didn't sleep all weekend. They will also not get away with sleeping during planned program during the retreat days. If they are taking responsibility for their nights, they will have to take responsibility for their days. Sleep is also a self-regulating behavior although it is a bit more long-range than eating. Experienced retreat goers tend to be more realistic about their sleep needs.

3. Smoking

Rules vary with who is going—maturity, age, culture, and commitment.

Although we do not encourage smoking, we generally try to make it possible for those who smoke, high school age and up, to have a place where they can smoke away from the rest of the group. (Of course, there is no transportation to restock a depleted supply.) In working with youth who are not Christians, we feel it is counterproductive to raise minor issues with them when that issue could block the real message and experience of the love of Christ which we want to share. We cannot demand a complete change in behavior before a person has made a commitment to follow Christ. We feel it is more important to demand adherence to other ground rules than to a "no-smoking" rule.

On one occasion, at a facility where smoking was against the rules, an exception was made for two emotionally disturbed girls (from a state institution) who were constantly sneaking away to smoke. Giving permission in regulated circumstances made it safer for all.

When the group is junior high age and smoking is not an ingrained habit but a matter of experimentation, we have the policy of checking with parents to confirm their permission for their teen to smoke. Just the intention to check with parents usually calls the experimenter's bluff who is maintaining, "My parents know and it's OK."

The basic issue is one of long-range health. By example and guidance we hope to encourage youth to take care of the *temples* of their spirits.

4. Drug Abuse

It is a generally accepted rule of most groups that there will not be any alcohol or other drug usage except by doctor's prescription. (Of course, this excludes the socially acceptable drugs: coffee, tea, soft drinks, etc.) For any lengthy retreat the registration form should ask: "Are you on any special medication? Give the name of your doctor and the name of medication."

If a person has a special health problem, such as epilepsy, diabetes, etc., someone, if not all the staff, should be briefed by the youth or his/her parents on what steps to take in case of an emergency, and what are the signs of an impending attack. If an attack occurs, accept and deal with other group members' reactions (curiosity, fear, repulsion, concern). Otherwise there is no need to treat the person with "kid gloves" or make special exceptions for him/her.

If word comes to you that someone on the retreat has drugs along, THEN is the time to deal with the issue. If only one person who is an "isolate" from the main group is involved, then it would not be appropriate for a total group discussion. When the group is aware and a number are experimenting or using, then it IS time to deal with the issue as a total group—no matter what the regular preplanned program/schedule calls for.

Andrew Weil's book, *The Natural Mind* (Houghton Mifflin, $2.95), is an excellent presentation of users' motivations and levels of dangers of all the various drugs.

Case Example: Our first rumor of illegal drugs was unverifiable; so it led to the following inclusions in the morning worship. Small groups discussed: "You are on a retreat with a group of high school youth from an area church. It is rumored that some are smoking marijuana on the retreat. You, as the leader, do not know who the smokers are and cannot verify the rumor. (1) If such a rumor were true and word of it leaked out to the home church, what might be some of the consequences for the future of the group? (2) As the leader responsible for this group, what problems would be raised for YOU if the rumor were true? (3) If the love of God is our basis for meeting, what does this action mean for one group? (4) What do you think the leader should do?"

Each question was asked separately and ten minutes or so was allowed for discussion. The conversation was lively and VERY realistic. The groups shared their conclusions. The leader's final statement closing this portion of the worship service was, "It will be my assumption that there will be no drugs on any future retreats or group trips. You know the reasons why!"

It was nearly nine months before the drug problem surfaced again on a retreat. Several youth were smoking grass out behind a building. Two of them had been on the previous retreat where the above discussion was held. Questions were put to them and to the group: "What do you think the leader should do? What do you think is fair in this situation?" The youth did not want this responsibility and therefore said, "You decide. Tell us what is going to happen. Get it over with." No solution was reached after an hour, and it was already 1:00 A.M. We set the date to finish the discussion for the following Tuesday afternoon.

Conclusions on Tuesday were: "If there are any further incidents, no questions will be asked, and those members involved will be taken home to their parents with a full explanation to them of the reasons why we are there." Our intention was to help the youth face their own behavior and its consequences, to help parents in dealing with their young people, and to protect the life of the group so it could continue to exist as a tool for God to use. Again the issue was raised in a regular group meeting with role playing of several "hypothetical situations," and the "new policy" with consequences was clearly stated.

You guessed it. The leaders were tested a couple of months later, and several youth were taken home to their parents. It was a painful growing experience for all of us. Some parents did not even know that their young folks smoked at all, let alone grass. Several parents who were angry initially came to us later and thanked us for caring enough about them and their young people to bring them the news and help them deal with it.

Parents were involved as a family unit with the youth. The meetings turned into communication sessions clarifying a lot of family tensions and issues. A good idea, never implemented, would have been for several sets of parents to get together with their youth for some joint sessions.

Referral was made in several instances to a Christian psychologist, and a group was established for a time for the youth involved. They went weekly and paid for a portion of the cost themselves, with parents and the church also paying a portion.

Note: Alcohol is a slower acting drug in terms of the health toll, but is the most damaging of all addicting drugs. We would take similar steps with anyone who was drinking alcohol.

5. **Sex**

Guys and gals like to be together. Teens are experimenting with patterns of intimacy and with powerful new drives and body changes. Making room in the program for this significant growth activity changes the atmosphere from one of "sneaking around" to one of permission to explore with guidelines and limits.

Allow for some free time for couples to be together, within a caring structure. Provide a place for late night fellowship with supervision. Even have a slumber party! These are just suggestions. Many groups incorporate body contact activities in a group setting—games, hayrides, swimming. Retreat programs have been designed to explore boy-girl relationships.

More importantly, the leaders' modeling and their own attitudes toward their bodies can influence youth. Young people notice when adults share their delight in their bodies as temples for God and self and for sharing love with others.

If word comes to you that a couple has been engaging in sexual intercourse, you must first check the information out. In our experience, when discussion with the couple verifies the rumor, we would ask if intercourse is a regular part of their relationship or if the occasion on the retreat was unusual. In addition to stimulating their sharing about the meaning of their relationship, we would inquire regarding the use of contraceptives and their attitudes about possible consequences. Then we would be sure the girl went for a pregnancy test. If she were not pregnant, the information about their intercourse might not need to be shared with parents, depending upon the couple's attitude, and the seriousness of any identity problems. We would try to assist the couple in sorting out their feelings toward each other and the future of their relationship. If the girl has become pregnant, we would meet again with the couple to assist them in sorting out their feelings toward themselves, their relationship, the child to come; and the alternative actions available to them. (Marriage may or may not be a viable alternative.) Then we would help them decide and plan what they will do and how to tell their parents. Much follow-up with the individuals and with the families would then be involved. If you decide you don't have the time or the competence to follow through, appropriate referral should be made.

A homosexual experience might not necessitate all the same steps in that no potential children are involved and the circle of people directly influenced is therefore smaller. We would spend time discussing with those involved what they seek in relationships, the meanings for them, their attitude toward themselves, and potential consequences. Masturbation may also be seen as a problem by some. It certainly is if done publicly, which is when this activity might come to light. Guilt over masturbation, or the use of masturbation as a regular means of avoiding relationships with others, is a problem which can be handled through counseling.

Referrals to a qualified counselor may be in order for anyone seriously disturbed by his/her sexual activity.

6. **Privacy**

People have a right to privacy; most people want some territory of their own. In a retreat setting where people are living closely together, it's fun to share and yet there are times needed for personal duties and elbowroom.

On youth retreats we have usually let the youth handle their needs for privacy during the daytime and then have assisted with guidelines about separate sleeping quarters as the sun goes down. Exceptions to this can be made if the group is sleeping out under the stars or is having a supervised slumber party.

And then there are always RAIDS which are so popular, especially among the younger teens.

We do not encourage raids. However, we accept them and deal with them as they arise. We encourage leaders to "sell-it-down" when the raid idea comes up in their cabin. However, the excitement and lure of this particular late-night adventure, often with the mystique of getting in to the girls' quarters, or proving one's power over another group of guys often overweighs the counselors' wet-blanket technique.

If the leader sees that his group is determined, and if the total group of leaders has decided to allow raids, then the leader with the group should develop clear limits regarding: OK "weapons" (clear water, shaving cream, frogs, bugs, etc.); territory; and the cleanup requirement.

We have found that once a group gets a crack at a raid, there is usually no great interest in raiding at future retreats because individuals find new ways to express their interest in power and in the opposite sex.

For dealing with raids when other groups are involved, see page 79. If your group members want a friendly raid on another group sharing the same facility, tell them that they can't do it now; but that you will check with the other group's leaders to see if they would have any objections. If there are no objections, the other group's being ready will make it more fun; if they are not interested, then your group will have to come up with another alternative to the raid. (Sometimes a midnight hike can be just as exciting as a raid.)

7. **Fighting**

Physical fighting is part of the culture of some folks and is the acceptable way of settling arguments. It is desirable to encourage youth to find more constructive ways of engaging in battle so that each of them emerges as a winner, and no one loses.

When/if physical fighting does break out between individuals, one strategy is to separate the fighters from the rest of the group and from each other. This may take brute strength and usually male leadership. Attempt to clarify the issues and angry feelings, helping the fighters find verbal expression. When they realize that their feelings are being taken seriously, that in itself may end the fight. If not, make it clear that they may continue to fight only if they will both sign an agreement to follow these ground rules: (1) They will fight fair using no objects, no kicking, and no hitting below the belt. (2) When the fight is finished, it is settled; there will be no escalation or getting buddies into the act later. Some will choose to fight. Others, with the temporary stop in action and the *separation from* the total group, will cool down and decide the fight is not worth it.

Follow-up in encouraging bridges to be built between the enemies is needed. Sometimes after the release of the power struggle, the fighters become friends. Honest engagement, even if conflicting, is preferable in our eyes to game playing and manipulation. The handshake and other symbols of acceptance and reconciliation can be encouraged.

Depending on the fight's issues and other group circumstances, there may be need for the total group to be involved in discussion and role playing around the issue of settling differences and dealing with conflict.

8. Stealing

It is often easier to ignore the offense of stealing than to deal with it.

The motivation for the act of stealing needs to be taken into account. Again in some subcultures the sense of property is defined differently than in the mainstream.

In general, a stolen item needs to be returned to its owner. If no one admits to the act, assuming the item is very valuable, then a statement to the group that everyone will face the consequences, unless the item is returned by a certain time, may be effective. If the item does not turn up, then the whole group can negotiate how it will set things right with the person wronged.

If an offender is identified, he/she should be given an opportunity to reflect upon his/her actions and decide (with the person wronged) which way he/she can make the wrong right—often by apology and return of the item. If the stolen item is lost or destroyed, the person can find other ways to make amends, such as giving the owner something of equal value or working for money to pay for a replacement.

CONCLUSION

Some of these problem areas are highly controversial. You may choose to handle them quite differently, or you may never have to deal with many of these areas. These methods of approach have worked well for us. Perhaps you can apply some of them to your particular situation.

Problems which have arisen on our retreats have been some of the most difficult and yet most growth-producing times for all involved. We are thankful for these times when people rub edges, when human caring is tested, and when the inflow of love from God heals and changes people.

With God's help, problems and people can be transformed.

24. Evaluation

Why evaluate? He who does not evaluate may not learn from the past and may make the same mistakes again in the future.

Evaluating involves gathering people's feeling and thought reactions to what has happened to see to what degree the desired goals have been accomplished. What happened of value? Without goals that have been clarified at the outset, evaluation loses its *yardstick* and turns into a gathering of individual feeling responses which may not accurately reflect the whole of the experience. An incident of painful feelings may have been a redemptive experience in the long run, and yet may be recorded negatively in evaluation if some "overviewing" elements are not included in addition to immediate feelings.

EVALUATION IS HARD. In a time of forward motion it is sometimes hard to make ourselves stand still and reflect on what has happened. Evaluation is like cleanup and countdown, making us realize the retreat experience is nearly over. If honestly done, the evaluation will force us to face problems we would rather overlook because we do not like to see mistakes or imperfections. It can also be a time of celebration of the good things which happened, renewed commitment, and a chance for resolution of conflicts. It is a way to integrate our learning back into the nitty-gritty of everyday life. It is a source of information for future retreat planning and directions in ministry.

Even ways of evaluating need evaluation. That is what this chapter is about.

WHAT NEEDS EVALUATION?

On a retreat, the elements which need evaluating vary according to the program, schedule, and type of leadership and planning process. Evaluation can be simple or quite inclusive. For the group which wants to do a thorough job, here are some elements which can help participants integrate their experience and provide information helpful in planning future action:

1. What I liked best . . .
2. What I liked least . . .
3. What I learned
   about myself . . .
   about the group . . .
   about God . . .
4. The element of the program which was
   most meaningful . . .
   least meaningful . . .
5. Activities which needed
   more time . . .
   less time . . .
6. New friends which I made . . .
   New enemies . . .
7. The leaders were (always, usually, seldom):
   prepared?
   fair?
   consistent?
   understanding?
   skilled?
8. I had a _____ voice in decision making
   (large, small, no)
   I wanted more?   less?
9. I saw myself being these (check as many as apply):
idea person	gatekeeper
humorist	starter
reconciler	questioner
synthesizer	information person
special pleader	opinion giver
opinion seeker	evaluator
summarizer	follower
doer	aggressor
counselor	blocker
encourager	other

   I wanted more to be: _____.
10. How could the facilities have been better?
11. Did you like the food? Did you like the way it was handled? Suggestions:
12. Were you satisfied with the sleeping arrangements? Suggestions:
13. How about transportation?
14. How could you have gotten more for your money?
15. How could resources and equipment have been better handled?

16. What did you understand the goals of the retreat to be?
17. How well did the retreat accomplish them?
18. I came on this retreat because. . . .
19. How well were your personal hopes met?
20. As I return home, I intend to be or do differently:
21. Three things I'd like to share with others about the retreat are:
22. Any further comments or suggestions:

These are elements that both leaders and participants can fruitfully consider! Leaders might obtain additional benefit by doing the following exercises of observation:

1. Take time to think about each individual in the group. What did I learn about him or her? Can I notice any change or growth?
2. What occurred in the group interaction? Cliquishness? Mingling? Emerging of new leaders (social, recreation, study, task)? Power struggles? Floundering? Effective leadership? Small group unity? Large group unity? Any loners?
3. Read over the participants' evaluation sheets and draw conclusions regarding what worked well and what new things should be tried.

For other elements worthy of reflection (for example, self-rating scale for leaders, rating of change, personal growth chart), see Leypoldt, *Learning Is Change*.[1]

For samples of two evaluation sheets which differ in specificity and complexity, see Appendixes 19 and 20.

HOW TO EVALUATE

Having a *written* evaluation form for individual reaction is only one way of doing the evaluation.

Silent reflection time and then verbal sharing, making use of a person or tape recorder to record the major points, can be very effective. This method has the advantage of the whole group getting more immediate feedback on individuals' thoughts and reactions. With the written evaluation form, all too often the group leaders are the only ones who get the overview of the feedback.

Other ways of getting information for evaluating, such as videotaping or appointing an observer(s) who has designated observation categories, are more effective for short activities during the retreat than for the entire retreat experience. Evaluation of group process in such instances can be part of the retreat programming.

Conducting interviews in radio or TV style or using tape recorders can be effective ways of securing individual reactions. This is a fun method but tends to capture immediate and "on-the-spot" types of reactions, leaving out feedback which could arise from lengthier and more solitary reflection time. Having people meet in twos or threes for sharing and then reporting to the larger group can work well.

Leaders and/or group members may want to do a ranking exercise which can give the group feedback on the amount of interaction, kind of leadership, and amount of cohesiveness in the group.[2] This feedback is not the type to unload on the group just before leaving the retreat setting. It carries an emotional weight, arousing people's fears and hopes in questions of rejection, popularity, power, and acceptance which need time and energy for resolution. This ranking tool, if used during the retreat, can give leaders a chance to examine their own patterns of contact with participants and make a change if needed.

Bernie Linnartz, Youth Minister at Westminster Presbyterian Church in Springfield, Illinois, offers this idea for doing evaluation which he has found workable for junior/senior highers:

Use about an hour and divide the group into fourths; have each small group spend 15 minutes in each of the four areas:

[1] Martha M. Leypoldt, *Learning Is Change* (Valley Forge: Judson Press, 1971), pp. 132-148.
[2] See Leypoldt, *op. cit.,* p. 126.

Area I—Write poetry, using the theme word.

Area II—Pick out a picture from magazines to say what you feel about the retreat; have a sharing time (taped).

Area III—Each person brainstorming for new ideas for future retreats.

Area IV—Each person writes a few words about: place, program, adult-sharers.

He also feels that additional time is needed to talk about and plan for reentry into the home/church situation.

If you decide to evaluate with the written evaluation form, consider the following suggestions. The way the form is worded can influence the type of feedback received. Open-ended statements or questions (other than "yes"/"no" types) leave room for unpredictable responses not envisioned by the developer of the form. Questions which have multiple-choice answers can limit the range of response. Forms with specific categories for response can stimulate the memory: "Oh, yes, I do have feelings about that." The form can give permission for registering negative feelings by asking specifically for them or by using a ranking scale which includes negatives (Appendix 20).

The oral or written statements accompanying the distribution of the forms can set the tone for a serious, honest, caring, reflecting instead of just a quick cleanup duty.

WHEN TO EVALUATE?

Evaluating activity can be part and parcel of the program and hence be done during the retreat, especially if the retreat goal is group-building, planning for the future of the group, or perhaps personal growth. Evaluating the effectiveness of any kind of retreat can be done beneficially at several different times.

In a longer retreat, a daily "tell-it-like-it-is" session for all participants may be effectively used, providing opportunities for the spontaneous happenings and the working of the Holy Spirit to be incorporated into the rest of the retreat. Some groups do a rehash after each major program element as a way of integrating, celebrating, and resolving conflicts before moving into the next event. Chapter 11, on Leadership, mentions the need for structured time for leaders to gather to evaluate. However, be aware that groups can "overevaluate," like the anxious gardener pulling up the turnip every few minutes to see if it has grown, thus not allowing the conditions for growth to develop. Evaluating produces self- and group-consciousness which can be inhibiting if overdone. As gardeners of human life we need to experiment to find the balance for ourselves and our

group to find the appropriate rhythm between doing and reflecting.

In general, for a weekend-length retreat, one whole group evaluation session during the retreat makes sense. Leaders and committees may evaluate progress more frequently.

An effective timing is prior to or during the closing worship service. This timing allows for the learnings, feelings, conflicts, and growths to be lifted up more consciously to God, and his power felt in reconciliation, redemption, and proclamation. A campfire or candlelight focus often can encourage a deepened concentration for reflection and be a magnetic pull for sharing.

Many retreat planners wait until after returning home for the feedback session. Participants gain the perspective of time but perhaps lose some of the freshness of feeling response. Also it is sometimes more difficult to ensure the presence of all those who were on the retreat.

We like to take advantage of both timings. We do some evaluating during the retreat to stimulate responsiveness and a feeling of closure in order to ease the transition to going back home. The evaluation done at the home front forms the rest of the bridge from "what has been" to "what is to be."

HOW CAN EVALUATION BE USED?

Make a summary sheet describing the retreat and incorporating the evaluation for the permanent church files. See the sample summary form, Appendix 21.

Evaluations are valuable sources of the following information:

1. effectiveness of resources, facilities, menus, type of transport, schedule, leaders
2. issues of concern to the group for future discussion
3. recognition of new skills, talents, and interests
4. problems which are traceable to inadequate planning
5. unforeseen problems which arose which could be taken into account in future planning

Evaluations are structured ways of making use of the new information gained from the retreat for choosing new behaviors to accomplish more fully the goals of your group. EVALUATIONS ARE STIMULI TOWARD CHANGE. The changes may not only refer to future retreat planning, but also to ways of carrying out the ongoing group life for which the retreat is but a vehicle. An example of a new direction stimulated by a retreat is that one retreat experience pointed to the need for increased contact of youth with parents, and so we set up more programs in family ministry—parent-teen communication workshops and cross-generational interest groups (photography and drama). We also felt the need to develop a questionnaire which would involve the parents in the retreat evaluation process.

OVERVIEW EVALUATIONS

Evaluations need not be limited to one retreat at a time. It may be helpful in a group's life to examine the trend of its retreating to break out of the rut which precedence so often sets. How frequently this kind of evaluation is done, of course, depends on the number of retreats taken in any one year and for what length of time group membership and/or leadership is stable. It may make sense for boards which have an annual retreat to evaluate the overall trend once every three years. Youth groups who usually do more frequent retreating might benefit from an overview evaluation every two years. See Appendix 22 for a sample evaluation form.

The Alpha and Omega of the planning process, the connection in the circle, evaluation is the taking seriously of Christian goals and people-happenings and fitting them together. Potentially in its finest form

EVALUATION IS

a form of meditation,

a crossing-point of the divine and the natural,

a fire for change,

a purging, reconciling process where pain and destructive forces can be transformed into health and light!

25. Reentry

AFTER THE RETREAT, "Whew! We can rest!" The time pressure and intensity is off, but the retreat is not yet finished.

REENTRY ACTION includes:

1. Completion of evaluation and record keeping with retreaters
   a. Back-home evaluating
   b. Incorporating descriptions and findings into on-going group records (Appendix 21)
   c. Making decisions about changes in group's life.
2. Follow-up with conflict resolution when needed (See chapter 23 for How-to's)
   a. within group
   b. with family members
   c. with other church members.
3. Acknowledgment and thanks (in writing for those not in the immediate group) to all the people who helped. Are you remembering donors, drivers, cooks, outside leaders, staff at the facility who put forth special effort? A good retreat is a reward in itself, but take time to thank group members who worked hard.
4. Share the successful retreat with others by:

Word of mouth
Exhibiting photos, symbols
Sending a write-up for church newsletter
Giving a worship service
Proposing new action for church members/groups

Doing new action
Sending ideas to *Recycle*
Sending a report to your denominational headquarters for publication
Sending us a copy!

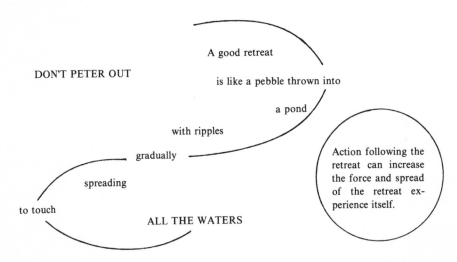

DON'T PETER OUT

A good retreat is like a pebble thrown into a pond with ripples gradually spreading to touch ALL THE WATERS

Action following the retreat can increase the force and spread of the retreat experience itself.

Section IV
Programs and Resources

Appendix

Planning-Process Resources

Worksheets

Sample Forms

Evaluations

Program Summaries

List of Resources

List of Contributors

Program Ideas Chart

1 SUMMARY OF OVERALL STRATEGIC PLANNING PROCESS
Larry Waltz

Step One: ASSUMPTIONS/GIVENS

I. Diagnose the situation

  A. What does the group need/want to do?

  B. What is the problem that needs to be solved?

  C. What are your overarching goals/purposes?

  (Write these out on newsprint for all to see.)

II. Gather data

  A. About you as leader:

    1. Are you excited about what the group wants to do? Why or why not?

    2. What do you hope will happen?

    3. What are your feelings, motives, commitments?

    4. To which goals are you committed?

    5. Will you (and how) give personal leadership?

  B. About the situation:

    1. How much time is available?

    2. When will event(s) be held? Where?

    3. What will the climate of the meeting be? Open? Comfortable?

    4. Who is responsible for developing what will happen?

    5. What resources and equipment are available?

    6. Who is sponsoring the event? Who is paying the bills?

  C. About the group:

    1. What skills are within your group? What added skills are needed?

    2. What is expected that the group will learn?

    3. On the basis of previous experiences, what is expected to happen at the event?

    4. What relationship exists between the group leaders and the group members?

    5. What leadership skills are there in the group?

III. Analyze data

  A. List all data and identify trends: Which items are similar? Which don't fit? What seems to stand out as a prime concern or priority?

  B. Rank priorities. You can't do everything.

Step Two: Write the OBJECTIVE

After completing the above steps, work one of the priorities into a specific statement of objective that gives consideration to a desired change in behavior, is measurable, and is attainable.

Step Three: STRATEGY/General Plan

  I. Brainstorm. What are the most creative ways you can reach your goal? Sort out ideas. What ideas have the most merit? Will they work? Is the goal exciting? Would YOU respond to it?

  II. Write a general plan statement on how you will meet your objective.

Step Four: TACTICS

  I. Details (every detail related to the event)

    A. List what is going to be done, how people are going to get on board. Plan for introduction and conclusion. Build in evaluation.

    B. Build a time schedule showing major blocks of time; who is responsible for meals, worship, recreation, free time, etc.

    C. List all materials, equipment, and resources you will need. Check out facilities.

    D. Determine the function of each member of the leadership team. Try a dry run.

  II. Do it

Step Five: EVALUATION

Evaluation can be written, verbal, or group observation by teams. Look at the goal; was it appropriate, clear, and concise to those present? Was it attainable? What could have been done to have had a better experience? Check out emotional reactions, information retained, changes of behavior, group process, and additional skills needed.

Record and summarize your evaluation for easy reference in planning another event.

(See Appendix 6 for a Goals Planning Work Sheet.)

2 QUICK PLANNING POSSIBILITIES

So you don't have much time to plan, and you still want

to have a retreat? It IS possible, but recognize that there are some limitations/assumptions.

If you are the right kind of person, you may be able to put the whole thing together in your head in an hour. *One person* assuming responsibility for making all the decisions and then telling/directing the group works well if that person is capable, and if the group trusts him/her to do all the decision making.

A couple of people can plan a retreat in one meeting if—

1. The basic organizational details are to be simple and you already have a place to use (church, camp, cabin, or home). Additional ease comes if someone else is planning the food, if food is going to be purchased out, or if someone else has already planned a program.

2. The primary goal is fun/fellowship and little serious programming is desired, and the place, food, and transportation are the primary details to be worked out by the planning group.

3. Families work out their own menus and eat separately or meet for "pot-luck." (Again assuming informal style, fun/fellowship goals.)

Quickly planned/executed retreats are fine now and then. If used exclusively, the group will miss out on potential opportunities for growth and leadership development. (See chapter 11 for discussion of leadership styles.)

3   SOME GOALS FOR GROUPS

1. To help individual (youth/adults) come to a saving knowledge of Jesus Christ.

2. To help persons identify individual strengths and weaknesses; experience God's love and acceptance, and appreciate the ways we complement each other; appreciate God's unique gifts to each person; practice developing potential.

3. To experience new ground rules upon which a loving, caring society can be based.

4. To provide a place to go where we (youth) can do our own planning and not be TOLD what to do; experience the pain and joy of doing it; experience success and growth in leadership ability.

5. To play: learn to relax and be as trusting children.

6. To provide a large block of time where youth and adults together can live out their values and build mutual appreciation.

7. To appreciate what it means to be part of a family,

and to practice personal communication skills.

8. To study major tenets of the faith and to understand and practice their application to our lives, community, and world.

9. To broaden one's base of experience; to do traveling which one might not ordinarily do.

10. To provide opportunity for worship/experimentation in celebrating life; for PRACTICE of prayer, meditation.

11. To provide opportunity for service in the name of Christ; to plan ways to minister to and through the institutions of our society, and to change those institutions to make them more responsive to human need.

4   SUCCESS LADDER FOR YOUTH PROGRAMMING

I. Pick what you think are the three most successful program types in each category and RANK them 1, 2, or 3.

A. 5 people meeting regularly for fun, Bible study, and deep sharing. _____

100 people meeting weekly for singing, Bible presentation, and games. _____

30 people in a group, with a central core of 5 who take responsibility for focused programming. _____

15 people in a group, with a core of adults and youth who take responsibility for focused programming. _____

B. Groups with:
regular weekly meetings/programs _____

programs every other week _____

once-a-month programs, day long or overnight _____

no large group meetings, small interest groups which meet regularly _____

C. Youth in the youth group who also attend Sunday morning worship and church school. _____

Church youth in the community serving in other Christian organizations. _____

Church youth in the community serving through non-Christian organizations, for example: rest homes, etc. _____

Youth in the youth groups who are NOT church

members or members of church families and do not attend worship or church school. ____

Youth trained for witnessing on the street. ____

II. Discuss ranking with one other person and then with the group to see the degree of consensus. What values were the basis for your choices?

5 LONG-RANGE PLANNING FOR YOUTH PROGRAMMING (Getting Started)

1. Graph your present group(s) and then your ideal for the group(s) on the table provided on the adjoining page. This may be done individually, by age group leaders, or by the total team.

2. Evaluate your ideal. What are the measuring rods?

A. Biblical:
   Twelve Disciples
   Body of Christ
   Gifts of Spirit
   Signs of Spirit
   Koinonia
   Power
   New Life
   Ambassadors
   Servants
   Celebration

   Isaiah 40
   Micah 6:8
   Amos
   Psalms 8, 24, 100
   Matthew 5:43 ff.
       16:24 ff.
       18:20
       22:37-40
   Mark 8:23 ff.
   Luke 10:25
   John 10:10
       13:34-35
       14:12
   all the parables
   Romans 5:8
       6:23
       14
   1 Corinthians 8, 13
   2 Corinthians 5:17
   Galatians 5:22
   Ephesians 4:11-13
   James 1:22 ff.
   1 John 4:20

B. Community:
   1. How does your ideal harmonize with that of others on your (youth) leadership team?
   2. How does it fit with the total church purpose and priorities?
   3. How many person-hours will it take to implement?
   4. How costly is it in resources?
   5. How relevant is it to the needs of your (youth) group?

3. Analyze the forces making your (youth) group(s) what they are at present.
   What is the history?
       Cycles
       Size
       Program content
       Style of organization
       Conflicts
   Who is in the group?
       Needs (age)
       Strengths
       Samenesses
       Differences
   Who are the leaders?
       Experience
       Style
       Number
       Confidence
       Skills
       Values
       Needs
   What are the present resources? (List them.)

4. What does your group(s) already have which if increased would move it toward your ideal?

   What new resources and people are needed to move the group closer toward that ideal?

5. Which specific small part of your ideal can you begin moving toward in the next three months?

   How?

REAL AND IDEAL (YOUTH) GROUPS

1. Graph your *ideal* group on the line between the extremes in each category.
2. Using another color or style of line, graph your group as you see it now.

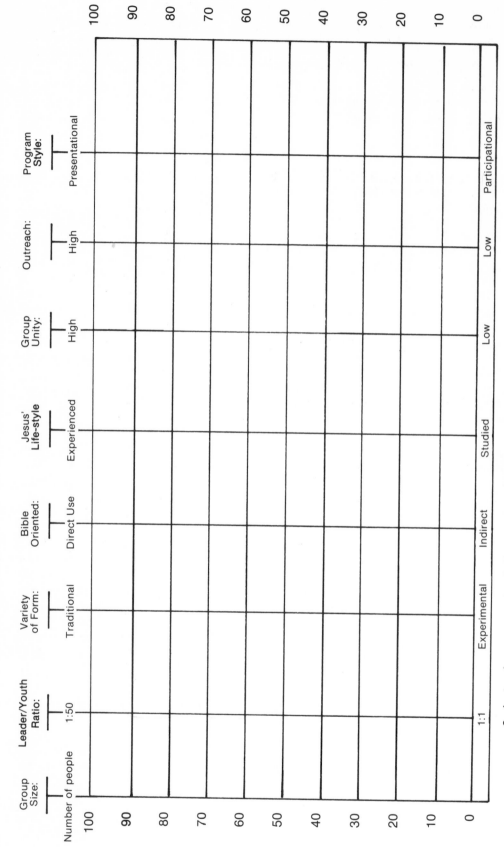

	Group Size:	Leader/Youth Ratio:	Variety of Form:	Bible Oriented:	Jesus' Life-style	Group Unity:	Outreach:	Program Style:
100	Number of people	1:50	Traditional	Direct Use	Experienced	High	High	Presentational
0		1:1	Experimental	Indirect	Studied	Low	Low	Participational

3. In two's compare and discuss your ideals/reals.
4. Graph the total group's reactions on one sheet and discuss.

6 GOALS/PLANNING WORK SHEET

GROUP:
DATE TODAY:

OUR PURPOSE
IS TO:

SO WE
WILL

SPECIFIC
OBJECTIVES

METHOD
(STEP BY
STEP EVENTS)

TARGET
DATE
TIME

WHO(SPECIFIC
PERSONS) DO
WHAT BY WHEN

RESOURCES NEEDED:
(**DOLLARS** + **PEOPLE** +
SUPPLIES)

(SEE APPENDIX 1)

7   GOAL ANALYSIS

INFORMATIONAL/CONCEPTUAL/COGNITIVE goals convey facts or concepts. For example, you might want a child to learn the Fifth Commandment: "Honor thy father and thy mother." If he/she can repeat it, then in a cognitive sense he/she "learned" it. Our churches are filled with people who have learned cognitive information but have NOT plugged it into their lives.

ATTITUDINAL goals strive for changes in feelings, attitudes, and values. The child who knows the commandment may still hate his/her parents. The goal here could be to provide opportunities/experiences aimed at giving him/her the opportunity to examine and change his/her attitudes. No one can force anyone to learn anything. A person may give "right answers," but in doing it, he/she may have "learned" to hate you, the church, or the school.

EXPERIENTIAL/BEHAVIORAL goals aim at providing the opportunity for practicing "doing" or "being" the new persons in Christ, or for increasing skills in a particular area. They may also attempt to be met through providing a setting where a person can experience the love of God in his/her life as opposed to talking about that love. A safe setting for experimentation with different behavior is also important if persons are to change.

The above categories are not mutually exclusive, but we often are not careful how we state our goals or how we use them.

The following exercise will give your group some practice in determining the KIND of category of goal statement which is listed. Note that each statement includes or assumes more than one particular kind of goal.

To create a "Goals Identification Worksheet," make copies of the following goals, without the parenthetical codes, for each member of the group. Ask each person to write in his/her definition of the goal, using "I/C" for informational/cognitive goals, "A" for attitudinal goals, and "E" for experiential/behavioral goals.

After each person has completed the sheet, have the members of the group compare their listings, first with one other person, then with the total group. Since these definitions may be a matter of judgment, even those suggested here are not necessarily the "right" answers, and discussion is in order.

1. To gain a sense of awe (A) for life as God intended it (I), to become aware of the implications (I/C) for persons to fill, control, and use God's creation.
2. To become sensitive to (I and A) the horror of war; to discover ways of living (I) and working for peace

as part of the church (would be "E" if the statement read, "to become involved in ways").

For further practice, your group may want to follow this same process with goals listed in Appendix 3.

Knowing the kind of goal helps to clarify which strategies would best achieve it.

8   EVERYONE CAN PLAN

(Sample planning process, using meal planning as model.)

One way to help people realize their planning abilities and to help them differentiate between the various phases or stages of the planning/goal-setting process is to ask the group to list everything which needs to happen to get food on the family table. Allow about four or five minutes. As people read their lists, begin to ask questions regarding the categories of their items. Develop and label categories.

Compare the developed list with the phases of the retreat or committee planning process as follows:

1. Goal: to get food regularly on the family table.

2. Givens/resources
   Assumptions
   Data gathering and
      ways to do it
   Evaluation

   (number of people: ages, likes/dislikes; dietary restrictions; dollars available; equipment: in kitchen, etc.; setting for meals: inside/outside)

3. Objectives

   (nourishing food; variety; hot meal at least one time a day)

4. Priorities

   (most important aspects for this time period)

5. List of what needs to be done
   a. division of labor

   (menu preparation; food listing and purchasing; cooking; serving; setting up; cleaning up)

   b. assignment of tasks

   (Who does what? When?)

6. Do the tasks

   and then EAT!

7. Evaluate (overall)

9 WORKSHEET ON PROBLEM SOLVING

1. Our most immediate problem with programming is:

   —Not enough prepared resources on hand
   —Lack of confidence on the part of leaders to use materials available
   —Difficulty getting from ideas to organization appropriate to need
   —Difficulty getting ideas for theme
   —Difficulty implementing program
      —Lack of time on adult leaders' part
      —Lack of time on youth leaders' part
      —Not enough interest on the part of youth
      —Difficulty making transitions from fun to serious
   —Not enough leaders
   —Other:

   (Is this problem a programming problem or one of leadership recruitment or training?)

2. List the forces which perpetuate the problem / Forces which counter the problem

3. Which of the above perpetuating forces would be easiest to lessen?

   Which of the above counter forces would be easiest to increase?

4. Choose actions to implement items identified in 3.
   Who?   Does what?   How?   By when?

5. How many person-hours do these actions take?
   If not realistic, choose another strategy, perhaps less ideal, but accomplishable.

10 ADVANCE QUESTIONNAIRE FOR NINTH AND TENTH GRADERS

1. Have you ever been to _____ (place) before? How many times? Type of retreat or camp? _____. What did you like best/least? _____.
2. What kinds of things do you enjoy doing in your spare time? (hobbies, etc.)
3. Complete the following sentences any way you would like:
   a. The thing I like best about myself is . . . .
   b. My biggest problem is . . . .
   c. The things I like the most about my church (or churches in general) are . . . .
   d. The things which bother me the most about my church (or churches in general) are . . . .
   e. I like school best when . . . .
   f. I don't like school when . . . .
4. Will you be bringing any equipment with you? (Super - 8 camera; cassette recorder; favorite record albums—two only; favorite book or magazine.) List please.

   Please drop in the enclosed envelope and mail!

11 SENIOR HIGH THEME BRAINSTORMING LIST
Potential Discussion and Theme/Issue Topics.

girls/boys; boy-girl relationships; flower power; pot and LSD; homosexuals, sexual freedom; new morality; beauty contests; playboy philosophy; politics, political candidates; SDS; Nazism; Black Power; United Nations; spirit world; ESP; UFO's; astrology; genetics; evolution; church and state; death; life after death; nuclear power; arms; third world war; Israeli war; U.S./U.S.S.R.; Vietnam; poverty; good movies; comedy; cartoon strips—theology/philosophy of life; medicine; mercy killing; marriage; problem pregnancies; abortion; obscenity; pornography; ecumenism; other denominations and religions; good things about our church along with problems; prayer; public/private; obesity; grades; the Trinity; Judaism; Jesus in the business world; mixed marriages; color; ethnic groups and racial riots; suicide; teacher/student relations; Bible authority, validity; atheism, fundamentalism; draft: dissension, C.O.; alternative service, choices between different branches of service; jobs; college; dropouts; parents/teens; women's liberation; speaking in tongues; white and black racism; faith healing; definition of sin; TV/media influence; transcendental meditation and altered states of consciousness; religious prejudice; visiting other groups.

12   PUBLICITY

Let your creativity flow. One planning group at Hatboro Baptist Church used a series of six "Peanuts" style cartoons drawn on 8″ by 11″ pieces of construction paper and posted around the church. One showed Lucy speaking to Charlie Brown. She is saying: "Charlie Brown, are you going on the BYF retreat? You'd better, because if you don't, you are going to miss an awful lot of fun." Charlie is shown thinking to himself: "Lucy doesn't know that I have already paid my $2.50 to Barbara Burger for registration."

13   RATING SCALE FOR SELF AND OTHERS

WHERE AM I? _____

WHERE DO I THINK (HE, SHE) IS? _____
(Use two kinds of marks: one for self and one for others.)

enthusiastic / / / / / / / / / / / nonplussed
    5 4 3 2 1 0 1 2 3 4 5
dependent _____ independent
moody _____ even-keeled
trusting _____ suspicious
irritable _____ easygoing
fearful _____ secure
confident _____ unsure
perfectionistic _____ casual standards
pushed _____ relaxed
humorous _____ straight
bossy _____ docile
forgiving _____ carrying a grudge
helpful _____ uncooperative
approachable _____ detached
energetic _____ tired
prying _____ hands-off
frank _____ deceitful
explosive _____ never gets angry
creative _____ dull
worried _____ carefree
happy _____ unhappy
aggressive _____ withdrawn
curious _____ nonexplorative
impulsive _____ disciplined

14   COMMUNICATIONS WORKSHEET

These questions are to be answered privately by teens and parents as noted and then shared. During subsequent discussions, each person should identify one area in which he/she will attempt change.

FOR TEENS:

A. Self:
1. Things I like most about myself are . . .
2. Things I like least about myself are . . .
3. I get angry at myself when I . . .
4. The things I would like to do most in life are . . .
5. One of the biggest mistakes I ever made was . . .
6. I need to . . .

B. Parents:
1. My mother is good at . . .
2. My father is good at . . .
3. My mother makes me angry when she . . .
4. My father makes me angry when he . . .
5. My parents always get angry when I . . .
6. My parents need to . . .

C. Family:
1. The biggest contribution I can make to our family is . . .
2. Our family needs to . . .

The specific issues or problems I would most like to discuss or see discussed during the sessions are . . .

FOR PARENTS:

A. Self:
1. (1-5 same as Self for Teens)
6. I feel the most pressure when . . .

B. Spouse:
1. The things I like most about my spouse are . . .
2. My spouse makes me angry when . . .
3. The biggest problems between us are . . .
4. My spouse complains about my . . .
5. The thing(s) I enjoy most in life is . . .

C. Family:
1. The biggest contribution I can make to our family is . . .
2. Our family needs to . . .

D. Son/Daughter:
1. The best thing about _____ is . . .
2. _____ makes me angry when . . .
3. _____ needs to . . .
4. _____ gets angry when I . . .
5. When he/she makes a mistake, he/she usually . . .
6. When he/she fails at something, I feel . . .

The specific issues or problems I would most like to discuss or see discussed during the sessions are . . .

15 SAMPLE MEDICAL AND HEALTH SHEET

Secure a copy for every person in your group. Keep the original at the church and make a copy to take with you on trips. If the trip copies are misplaced, many hours of trying to get new signatures can be saved. This form is patterned after the California code. You should check with your state's laws, or ask your church's attorney to do so. The law generally requires you to foresee possible medical problems and to secure parental consent for treatment.

MEDICAL CONSENT FORM

In the event that our child _____ becomes ill or sustains an injury while on an authorized and chaperoned outing from *(name, address of church)*, I, the undersigned, give my permission to those in charge to take whatever steps are necessary to stop any bleeding and to administer first aid.

I also consent to an X-ray examination, anesthetic, medical (or dental) or surgical diagnosis and treatment and hospital care, and the administration of drugs or medicine to be rendered to my child under the general or specialized supervision and upon the advice of a duly licensed physician and/or surgeon.

I understand that this consent will apply to all emergency situations present and future, and that a copy of this form is as valid as the original. This consent is to remain in effect until written revocation is made.

Date _____   _____
                          (signature of parent or legal guardian)
Address _____ Phone _____

ANY SPECIAL HEALTH PROBLEMS? Describe: Any medications? (name/dose/prescribing physician)

Regular doctor: Name _____ Phone _____

16 Sample Registration Record

	NAME	$2.50	$5.00	GROUP	ROOMMATE PREFERENCE	RIDING WITH
1.	Tom Hudson	X	X	Senior H.		
2.	Linda Ritchie	X	X	Junior H.		
3.	Leslie Jarrett	X		Junior	Barb Hobensack Claudia Hackney	
4.	etc.					
5.						

17 SAMPLE ROAD RALLY LOG

(from Hatboro, Pennsylvania, to Randolph, Vermont)

DATE: driver: co-driver: treasurer:

total number of miles: 425
estimated total driving time—9.5 hrs. at 55 mph.

CHECK POINTS:

	odometer	time	time en route	number of miles
1. Starting point: church _____	_____	_____	_____	_____
2. Toll booth at E. end of Pa. Turnpike	_____	_____	_____	_____
3. Toll booth of N.J. Tpk. N. on Garden State Parkway	_____	_____	_____	_____
4. Rest stop: (gas optional) north of Patterson, N.J., exit. Max. time 20 min.; min. time 15 min.	_____ _____	_____in _____out	_____	_____
5. Optional stops	_____	_____	_____	_____
6. Randólph, Vt.	_____	_____	_____	_____
Totals: overall time, mileage.			_____	_____

CAR EXPENSE LIST: (gas stops/tolls) cash at start—$25.

odometer	no. of gals.	$ per gal.	total cost	miles per gal.	TOLLS:
1. _____	_____	_____	_____	_____	1. _____
2. _____	_____	_____	_____	_____	2. _____

TOTALS upon arrival in Randolph, Vt.
Cash at start $25.00
Cost for gas: _____
Cost for tolls: _____
Total cost: _____
Balance to retreat treasurer: _____

Carload which comes closest to the suggested time, with best mileage, etc., gets a treat.

18   MENU SUGGESTIONS

SOME BREAKFAST OPTIONS:
(Every breakfast does NOT have to have "hot" food.)

juice: canned/frozen
fruit: fresh/canned, cantaloupe, grapefruit, oranges, bananas
Tang (expensive)
honey, brown/white sugar
milk: mix powdered milk to make ¼ to ⅓ of the total needed. (Served very cold, it is hard to tell difference.)
small amount of hot chocolate

sticky buns, rolls, toast/jam, cinnamon buns, muffins
hot cereal
cold cereal in individual boxes
pancakes
french toast
scrambled eggs

eggs to order for those who want them
bacon/sausage/
Spam fried in brown sugar/pineapple syrup, or make your own syrup: equal parts Karo brown/white sugar, water, maple flavoring.

LUNCH OPTIONS:

Sloppy Joes
hamburgers/hot dogs
peanut butter/jam sandwiches
lunch meat to make own sandwiches
tuna sandwiches
salads:
pick-up, tossed
fruit cocktail
cantaloupe
watermelon

grilled cheese sandwiches
soup: homemade/canned
stew
tacos or hoagies

Jell-O
cabbage, pineapple- marshmallow/orange
cottage cheese/tomato

onion, relish, etc., for hamburgers
juice-punch combination, milk, iced tea
pudding, fresh/canned fruit, potato chips
Fritos and dip, popsicles, ice cream
candy bar choice

DINNERS:

salads: similar to lunch.
baked ham, spaghetti, meat loaf, beef stew, pizza, french bread, corn on cob, frozen vegetables, baked potato, creamed chicken/biscuits, mashed potatoes, beans and hot dogs, apple sauce with cinnamon or hot candies, ice-cream, cookies, cupcakes/cake, cherry delight, pies from home.

SNACKS:

chips/dip, pretzels, punch, hot chocolate or cider, sodas, smores, marshmallow roast, hot dogs, popcorn, taffy pull, fresh fruit, cookies.

For further resources and menus, see your handy cookbook, Girl/Boy Scout camping manual, or write: "Recipes for Simple Outdoor Cookery," 25 cents, Board of Discipleship, United Methodist Church, Discipleship Resources, Box 840, Nashville, TN 37202.

SAMPLE SATURDAY BREAKFAST:
(Outline of Duties)
1. Set tables with milk, sugar, and butter on each table.
2. Set out on counter:
   a. cold cereal and bowls.
   b. juice (cans—open only two at a time).
   c. grapefruit—cut as needed, one at a time in advance.
   d. sticky buns—open one package of each at a time.
   e. paper plates.
3. Cooking duties:
   a. Heat water for coffee, tea (use Styrofoam cups).
   b. Make a small pan of oatmeal.
   c. Have skillet ready for egg orders.
4. Clean up—put food away, clear tables, wash dishes. Set up boxes for lunch meal.

19   SIMPLE EVALUATION
Mason Brown

1. What in the program has been most meaningful to you?   Least meaningful?

2. What personal growth have you made this weekend?

3. What would you like to see done another year?

20   EVALUATION: JOINT TRIP TO UNITED NATIONS:
Larry Waltz

Name: (optional)
Address:

Your candid and objective evaluation of our recent youth encounter tour is very important. Please indicate on the right a value figure for each area:

1 = excellent;   2 = good;   3 = fair;   4 = poor.

I. Evaluate the following areas:

Getting acquainted at Hatboro   ____
Small-group discussion (triads)   ____
Traveling in van to New York   ____
Living in the community house   ____
Rapping with "Vista" people   ____
Touring the U.N.   ____
Chinese dinner experience   ____

II. Personal feelings

Dealt with ideas about which you are personally concerned.   ____
Degree of freedom felt to express your personal feelings   ____
The degree of cooperation among group   ____
This model would interest others.   ____

III. Housekeeping items

Two-day event, versus a weekend retreat   ____
Importance of getting to know one another   ____
Cost for the event ($5 plus meals)   ____

IV. Please list your understanding of the objectives of the encounter tour.

V. List some items that you learned from this trip.

VI. List ways to improve this model.

VII. Additional comments.

Use this form as a guide in developing your own.

21 SUMMARY EVALUATION FORM FOR FILE

This form, or one like it, will allow you to find information quickly for future reference in planning. This sheet is *not* a substitute for the evaluation process; it is only a summary of the more pertinent information.

A. GENERAL INFORMATION

1. Group
2. Location of retreat
3. Dates
4. Age/sex of participants
5. Names of leaders
6. Special leaders
7. List of participants with leadership roles noted

B. COST SUMMARY

Income: Total money collected and amount from each
    Source of income: individuals
                       fund raising
                       other means
Expenses: Total expense
    Lodging, food, transportation, resources, persons, media, crafts, insurance, miscellaneous
Amount set aside for future resource purchases

C. EVALUATION (summary only here)

1. Goals/theme/program focus
2. Highlights of group process
3. Highlights of individual growth and commitment which were evident
4. General evaluation/reactions/feelings
5. Things that went well; things to do differently

22 SUMMARY EVALUATION FOR PARTICIPANTS FOR SEVERAL RETREAT EXPERIENCES

1. What retreats have you participated in?
   places   approximate dates
2. Did you help plan them?
   Which part did you do?
3. What things do you most remember?
4. What contributed to your spiritual growth?
   List specifics, if possible.
5. How did you feel about the handling of problems on the retreats?
6. What things bothered you the most?
7. What do you feel you still need to know (if anything) to help a group plan and carry out a retreat?

23 SCOTTSVILLE BAPTIST CHURCH JUNIOR HIGH RETREAT
Jim Foster

FRIDAY: (*Note:* schedule is in large time blocks.)

6:15 P.M.—Meet at Scottsville Baptist Church; 7—meet the Charlottesville group. 8:30—arrive at Buck Hill.
9:00—Begin group activities, tentatively including:

name game; contract; double circle using nonthreatening data; bubble exploration; double-bubble;

blind milling; trust circle; informal discussion and/or lecturettes; filmstrip: *Members One of Another;* snack before bed.

SATURDAY:

A.M.—Sleep; uncooked breakfast, RECREATION.
P.M.—Late lunch; afternoon activities:

fantasy experience   alone time
bubble exploration   blind walk

—LATE SUPPER:

double circle; depth involvement; strength bombardment or verbal encounter; caring symbolized through foot washing; fireside or candlelight tie-up.

SUNDAY:

A.M.—Sleep, uncooked breakfast.
Rocking; trust circle; searching dyads; alone time;
P.M.—Lunch; WORSHIP; EVALUATION; closing circle; leave for home by 3 P.M.

24   JUNIOR HIGHS: FRIENDSHIP
Bernie Linnartz

SATURDAY: 8:30 A.M.—Depart (arrive 10:30)

10:35—Total Group: state expectations and limitations; explain camp area: locations, camp rules, if any.
Determine and state living/meeting quarters.
Explain "Graffiti" and "message" boards.
Unpacking/exploring time.

11:15—*Friendship I*

Determine identity groups (See *Strategy,* March-May, 1974, for details); make name tags.
12:30 P.M.—Lunch
1:00—Organized volleyball/free time.

2:30—*Friendship II*

Role play: "new persons" situations.
Negotiation—two members to be switched from each group.

Feel out how "switched" persons feel.
Brief energy game.
Talk about "the Cage"; how we put people in cages; what cages are made of.
Free time.

6:30—Dinner

7:00—*Friendship III*

Movie: *What About THAD?*
Use newsprint to express feelings; use square on floor to let persons be Thad.
Talk about how Thad felt, how others could establish a relationship with him.
Brief energy game.
Movie: *Neighbors;* total group talk briefly about the film, what makes a good neighbor, a difficult neighbor. Free time.

9:30—Campfire: snacks, sing-along, worship, share.
11:15—In cabins; 11:45 lights out; 12:00 quiet.

SUNDAY:

8:00 A.M.—Breakfast

9:00—*Friendship IV*

Four areas (about 20 min. per area)
Four groups: Cinquain poetry; picture pick and ideas (tape-recorded); written evaluation: place, program, leaders, planning another retreat. Free time.
11:00—Clean up; pack up; free time.
12:30—Lunch
1:30—Closing worship/reentry thoughts.

25   RETREAT FOR GRADES 7, 8, 9
Montrose Bible Conference, Junior Highs at Hatboro Baptist Church

Some **GOALS** listed by the planning committee:
(If you can't do all, emphasize numbers 1, 4, and 5.)

1. to develop a better understanding of one another;
2. to add more members to the group;
3. to get a leader;
4. to gain more understanding of our Christian faith;
5. to plan for the rest of the year—topics, etc.

SESSION IDEAS:

FIRST SESSION: *Getting to Know Each Other Better.*

1. Potentials: What do we have in common? List the items. Get names.
2. Sharing in twos: "I am at my best when . . ."; "I am at my worst when . . ."; "I like people who . . ."; "I dislike . . ."; "I detest. . . ."; "I hope. . . ."
3. Trust: individual pairs, falling, blind walk,
4. How would you feel if—? (Describe on paper a problem or situation where you have felt hurt by someone else. Do not sign it. Drop all papers into a hat. Individuals pick one out; each tells how the person must feel. Combine with some role playing.
5. Closing circle; singing and sharing; potential movies: *The Nail; Neighbors.*

SECOND SESSION: *Our Relationship to God.*

1. Being a follower of Jesus is. . . .
2. Portrayal: God is like. . . .
3. Depth Bible study in small groups: (Create a way to share the meaning of the passage: role play, drama, skit, pantomime, paraphrase, etc.)
   Scriptures: Matthew 7 and others.

THIRD SESSION: *Worship.*
1. Singing
2. Sharing of Scripture/prayers
3. Circle prayer
4. Commitment/renewal
5. Celebration of Communion
6. Challenge of ministry in the world (movie: *The 60's;* discussion/feelings)
7. Closing circle.

26   MAKING GROUP MEDIA PRODUCTIONS
Bernie Linnartz

This weekend retreat was designed to provide input for group meetings in the future where the group would finish up, tie together, and complete the various productions begun on the weekend.

FIRST SESSION: Explore the idea of M.G.M. (Making Group Media); select possible scenes for taking pictures; and shoot one third of the scenery shots.

SECOND SESSION: Share experiences; form production groups; examine and choose media/method ideas:

Sample Topics:	Methods:	Media:
sports	commercials	slides
retreats	news items	movies
humor	interviews	tapes
friendship	weather	articles
worship	sports	posters

Begin to develop and design the productions.

THIRD SESSION: Lights/Camera/Action—put it all together on the drawing board and work on production and filming.

27   IN CHRIST, FREE TO BE
Youth Convention Camp-Out,
545 Senior High/College-Age Youth

GOALS: to create and develop a feeling of area and regional consciousness; to grow in our faith through Bible study, inspiration, and sharing. Program theme built around: Galatians 5:1, 13-15.

PROGRAM:

1. Get-acquainted activities and small-group Bible study by area. Scriptures: Galatians 3:28; 1 Corinthians 12:4-13, 27; 2 Corinthians 5:17-18; Luke 6:27-36; 1 John 3:17-18; 4:20; and 1 John 1:9. Members of each small group studied the meaning for them individually, for the church, and the world. They then created a way of illustrating/demonstrating the meaning of the Scripture, using role play, pantomime, drama, skits, interpretive movement, paraphrase, music, etc. Creations were shared within each area, and selected ones were shared with the whole regional group.
2. Total regional sessions included: speaker, music, sharing from Bible study groups, Sunday A.M. worship service, and Love Feast/lunch. (Rented a commercial PA system and generator; used 14 Coleman lanterns on poles for light at night.)
3. Area and regional recreation.
4. Cooking by individual churches or several churches combined; one whole area organized and cooked for over 80 persons in one place; most cooked for 15 to 20 persons.

28 CELEBRATION RETREAT FOR SENIOR HIGHS
Bernie Linnartz

I. *Celebration*
(Sounds; sights; talking about celebrations (New Year's, etc.); eating/drinking/rapping/singing; sharing celebration remembrances; writing out things to celebrate (ideas included in Program Ideas Chart).

II. *Celebration of Birth*
Do an imaginary journey of birth (on floor, eyes closed).
Do a thought journey (relax, clear mind)
—to a mountain, seashore, valley, sandy place; finding, lying on sand, sinking into sand, being tickled, being rocked by waves—soothing, etc.
—feeling the moisture of the earth, the warmth of the sun; growing, breaking shell of seed.
Awake: Welcome to the world. In groups of two or three talk about your experience.
Childhood: See the film *Wonder;* play the record "Celebration of Life." In small groups, talk about your childhood; think about things yet to be born: people, plants, animals, thoughts/ideas.

III. *Celebration of Death*
Music playing: "Abraham, Martin and John," "Turn, Turn, Turn."
In small groups talk about death experiences—family, pets, etc.
Movie: *A Time to Die*—share reactions.
Thoughts on resurrection: death to life—"Ballad of Easy Rider" (getting killed); "Rise Up, Easy Rider."
Poem written by J. Jones (in groups) "Sunset to Sunrise"

IV. *Celebration of Life*
Thoughts on being alive—breathing, heart beating, touching, holding hands, eyes meeting.
Movie: *Dancing Prophet*—talking about life. Interpretive dance: "Impossible Dream." Multimedia experience: "Hope."

V. *Celebration of NOW*
Fanfare for the common man (see Planning Chart). Balloons, music. Let it happen as long as it happens. Reflect/share.

**29 JOIN THE JESUS REVOLUTION
A Study of Jesus,
for Senior High Youth**
Bill Tallent and Don Baird

Basic focus for study/reflection on "Jesus People" using "Jesus Christ Superstar" and Scripture.

SATURDAY MORNING:

1. Listen to "Heaven on Their Minds."

   a. In small groups discuss how our concept of Jesus differs from that of Judas.
   b. Study Matthew 6:25; 18:31-34; 20:20-28; Mark 8:31-33; and 8:34-38.
2. Listen to "What's the Buzz?" Leaders comment.
3. Listen to "Strange Thing Mystifying" and "Everything's Alright." Small-group discussion of John 7:53–8:11; 11:1-8; Matthew 26:6-13; Mark 14:3-9; Luke 7:36-50, Matthew 25:31-45.
4. Listen to "This Jesus Must Die" and Matthew 26:1-5. In small groups, develop in ten minutes a two-minute skit depicting how we are threatened by Jesus and how we react by putting him down.

SATURDAY AFTERNOON:
1. Listen to "Hosanna" and sing it.
2. Listen to "Pilate's Dream" and leaders comment.
3. Listen to "Simon Zealotes" and "Poor Jerusalem" and have small-group discussion about today's parallels of politicians trying to use Jesus. See Psalm 46:1-7; Isaiah 14:32; Mark 11:10; Luke 19:41-44; Matthew 16:24-26.
4. Listen to "Damned for All Time" and "Blood Money." Provide two minutes for each person to think about what blood money means today; then discuss with the total group.

SATURDAY EVENING:
1. Singing/get-acquainted activities.
2. Listen to "The Last Supper"; sing "Gethsemane." Share feelings.
3. Small-group discussion of Matthew 25:31-46; Mark 14:32-42; Luke 22:39-46.
4. Light candles and place them in holders. Form a friendship circle with candles in the middle. Listen to "Peter's Denial," "Judas' Death," "Trial Before Pilate," "Crucifixion," and "John Nineteen: Forty-one." Read John 19:41; 20:24-29; and Matthew 28:18-20.
5. Have a quiet time for thinking. In small groups share feelings about the meaning of Christ for

me/us. Other possible questions: What is the meaning of the Great Commission for us? How do others respond? How should we? Are we ashamed of Jesus? How will people know we are Christians?

The retreat, using the musical as stimulus, precipitated a great deal of serious Bible study and focus on Jesus and the individual/group relationship with him and God. Personal renewal and a genuine commitment to work with one another in the groups were two profound results of the weekend of study and sharing.

30   CHANGE: SPRING RETREAT FOR SENIOR HIGHS
Betsy Bouska

Program folder given to each participant.
Material was adapted from Argus "Change" books.

GOALS:

1. To increase fellowship between youth of different churches and within each church.
2. To provide opportunity for learning in small groups led by the youth themselves.
3. To facilitate confrontation with the Christian experience of persons within the world and with others within the flux of change.

RESOURCE CENTER: Tape recorders, blank tapes, discussion tapes on "Change" from Argus.

31   OUR COUNTRY: RIGHT OR WRONG?
Gary Jenkins

FRIDAY NIGHT: (Arrival at 6:30 P.M)
   7:00   Food Team 1.
   8:00   Our Country—The Good Things
            Film, *An American Time Capsule*
            Discussion
   9:00   Games and get-acquainted time
  11:00   Devotions around the fireplace
SATURDAY: (Up and "attum" at 8:00)
   8:30   Appreciation time
   9:00   Food Team 2.
   9:45   Youth Programming and Planning
  12:30   Food Team 3.
   1:30   Our Country—The Extremes

            Film, *Is It Always Right to Be Right?*
            Discussion
   5:30   Food Team 2.
   6:30   Our Country—The Solution
            Film, *A Time Out of War*
            Discussion
   8:00   Free Time
   9:30   Saturday night at the movies, *A Raisin in the Sun*
  12:00   Lights out
SUNDAY: (Up and "attum" at 8:00)
   8:30   Food Team 3.
   9:30   Bible study in small groups
  10:30   Worship
  12:30   Lunch and free time
   3:00   Evaluation and camp cleanup
   3:30   Circle prayers; leave for home

32   FILM FESTIVAL RETREAT
Four churches in Muskegon, Illinois, area
Budget of $160, senior highs

FRIDAY EVENING: Violence and War

Films shown: *The Battle of Britain* and *The Soldiers*
Discussion following (no interlude between)

SATURDAY MORNING: Interpersonal Relations and Sex

The Game, shown to boys; *Phoebe* to girls.
Had separate discussions; then reversed showing of films to boys and girls

SATURDAY AFTERNOON: Violence and Poverty

Happy Birthday, Felicia and *The Church in the World* shown on center screen with two filmstrips on poverty/hunger shown on side screens

SATURDAY EVENING: Relaxing
The Chase
SUNDAY MORNING: Worship
It's About This Carpenter

33   RETREAT THEME: LOVE, AUTHORITY, AND DEATH

Retreat participants were given a 26-page pamphlet which included the selections listed below. The items were printed in many different directions on each page.

Materials were used in discussion, worship, and drama role play during the retreat and later on as well.

GOOD NEWS REGARDING AUTHORITY

First page:

A. "Ideally it would be great to have a closer relationship with my parents. I don't talk to them too much . . . though. . . . We're sort of outsiders right now." (*Discovery in Word,* p. 25.)

B. Cartoon from *New Yorker* (1965) with a girl saying to a guy in the picket line, "My mother probably thinks we're out necking or something."

C. See Mark 11:28: "What authority do you have for doing these things, and who gave you permission?"

Second page:

A. Words to "She's Leaving Home" from Sergeant Pepper's album by the Beatles.

B. Text of Ephesians 6:1

C. Playlet 7: "A Little Noise Never Hurts" from *Discussion Starters for Youth Groups, Series Two.*

D. Teenagers are torn between two different worlds. Especially toward parents they feel:

Nobody understands me.	But don't try to understand.
Don't give me directions.	But tell me what to do.
Why don't you love me?	But they love me too much.
Why don't they spend more time with me?	But leave me alone.
Why don't they talk to me?	But I won't listen to them.
Why don't they treat me more like an adult?	But they expect too much of me.
Why don't they let me be alone to be myself?	But who am I?

Third page:

A. Jules Feiffer cartoon with the caption, ". . . after all these years, what a discovery to make—we never liked children."

B. Joshua 24:24 (RSV): "The Lord our God we will serve, and his voice we will obey."

Fourth and fifth pages with similar material.

Sixth page:

A. Words to the song "Old Enough" by Ric Maston, from 12 String Sermons Album, PCDUUA, 2441 LeConte Ave., Berkeley, CA 94709, $6; "Too young to . . . but old enough to die."

B. With "big daddies" watching, the road of behavior is straight and narrow.

C. "Civil Authority, Church Authority, and Little People," from *Wine in Separate Cups,* ed. Charles Sauer and John Cooper (FEL Church Publications Ltd., 1925 Pontius Ave., Los Angeles, CA 90025), pp. 108-109.

Seventh, eighth, and ninth pages with similar material.

GOOD NEWS CONCERNING DEATH

Seven pages of material were created, using the following materials and sources:

Ecclesiastes 3:1; Matthew 22:32

Do You Hear Me, God? (pages 75, 81, 24, 43, 66-67).

For Mature Adults Only (pages 3-4).

Revelation 3:15

Songs "I've Got to Get a Message to You," from BeeGees, and "In the Ghetto" by Elvis Presley

2 Corinthians 4:11-14

Free to Live/Free to Die (page 20).

Wine in Separate Cups (page 94).

Are You Running with Me, Jesus? (pages 20, 60, 103).

Song "Who's Waving?" by Ric Maston.

Deuteronomy 30:15; John 10:10; Ecclesiastes 3:20; John 12:25.

34 **YOUTH EXCHANGE**
(Stoney Fork, Pennsylvania, and Ridley Park, Pennsylvania)
J. Minear and Larry Dobson

RIDLEY PARK TO STONEY FORK:

1. Tour Pennsylvania grand canyon; hike to bottom.
2. Tour strip-mining, have discussion of problems.
3. Youth banquet at church; film/discussion.
4. Old-fashioned hayride.
5. Sunday morning worship at the church.

STONEY FORK TO RIDLEY PARK:

1. Roller skating.
2. Tour of ABC headquarters and Valley Forge Park.
3. Tour of inner-city slums (Philadelphia).
4. Film: ghetto problems (city and suburban).
5. Tour radio tower of Philadelphia International Airport.
6. Meals in homes/worship Sunday at church.

35 **GOOT I and II.** (*Get Out Of Texas*)
J. Junke and G. Oswald

BASICS: 13 days; rented VW vans; $75 per person (1973). ($40 transportation; $12 food; $6 lodging; $8 canoeing; $9 miscellaneous.)

ITINERARY:

1. St. Louis: stayed in Concordia Church, visited synodical people and places: Board of youth ministry,

school of nursing, medical center, headquarters, seminary. (2 days)

2. Chicago: Hyde Park Lutheran Church, for values-clarification study, visits regarding city problems and needs. (3 days)

3. Ozark Scenic Waterway; Alley Spring's camp near Eminence, Missouri, canoe trip. (1 day)

4. Bull Shoals, Arkansas, State Park Lodge: hiking, caving, back-packing, folk arts, and crafts.

OTHER: Menus and meals prepared by the youth; plenty of time for focused discussion and worship in addition to what happened spontaneously in the van groups.

36 CRUISE *(Christian Renewal Underway In the Sailing Experience)* Rev. Conrad Braaten.

BASICS: One week's sailing experience, maximum 18 people; crew divided into "watch groups" of 6 to cook, 6 to sail, etc. Cost—$165 per person. (Write for a complete brochure; it may be available on the West coast of Mexico soon. c/o Biscayne Lutheran Church, 7610 Biscayne Blvd., Miami, FL 33138.)

INCLUDES: Opportunity for spiritual growth and study. Learning to sail the ship; *CIRCLING* (a sharing process in which each person talks one at a time, as long as he or she wants, sharing where he/she "is at" or what he/she is feeling. If a person does not want to talk, he/she "passes." The sharing continues around the circle until everyone has "passed" two times. The group does NOT respond to any person's sharing until the total group has finished the whole process. THEN there is opportunity to respond/celebrate what has been shared).

37 WEEKEND WORK CAMP David Richie October–May each year; fifteen years or older.

EXCERPTS FROM BROCHURE:

Whether you are ready or not, *you do face* a world of white and black racism; affluence for some, embittered poverty for others, exacerbated by broken promises, police brutality, and the apathy of so many of the affluent. Are you going to DIG A HOLE and then try to crawl into it? OR are you ready to DIG FOR TREASURE for yourself AND OTHERS?

Treasure! What TREASURE?

The joy of significant social involvement; new friendships, new awareness, maturity, self-confidence; new purpose. Write to 1515 Cherry St., Philadelphia, PA 19102.

DIG IN!

FRIDAY:

6:00—Supper, get acquainted with one another. Orientation: discussion with community people about the community: needs, residents, perspectives, projects, who the workers are. Organization of work teams.

SATURDAY:

7:30—Breakfast.

8:00—Twos and threes—with brushes, ladders, and lunches—work on community projects, paint, fix.

6:00—Supper. Rap and relax.

SUNDAY:

7:00—Breakfast.

8:30—Visit magistrate's court and urban redevelopment areas. Attend local city churches for worship or Friends meeting.

1:15—Dinner and final Rap: "What MORE?"

38 ECUPAX YOUTH EVANGELISM SEMINAR

An interdenominational conference including small group discussion, staffed by youth leaders.

1. Read Matthew 16:13-17. What does this account say about Christ?

2. Make a drawing representing your relationship to God.

3. Fill in the blanks to create a "cinquain" (sin-cane).*

_____ (title)

_____ _____ (description)

_____ _____ _____ (action)

_____ _____ _____ _____

(feelings)

_____ (one word summary)

4. Share your drawing and cinquain with others asking:

   a. What is there about Christ that appeals to you?

   b. How does Christ exemplify the love of God?

   c. What can we say about CHRIST in a positive way to give new insights to people?

   d. How can we demonstrate our faith in *action*, personally? As a group of youth? As congregations?

   e. What activities could you do to show others your commitment to Christ?

5. Personal witness commitment: In the light of what Christ means, I feel that my personal witness for him might be. . . .

The afternoon groups sessions lasted for just over an hour. Program included total group singing, worship, presentations, buffet dinner, and a candlelight procession to the cathedral for closing prayer service.

*Cinquains can be the form of expressing thoughts/feelings on any theme or subject. Have you tried them in your group?

39 EVANGELISM
Harold Schock

FRIDAY EVENING: Biblical Basis for Personal Evangelism

1. Lecture (30 minutes): Group evangelism in Nineveh— Jonah; general missions—Paul; to the Gentiles— Peter.
2. Discussion (30 minutes) focused on who, what, when, and where—in the following passages relating to personal evangelism: John 3:1-16, John 4, and Acts 8:26-40.

SATURDAY MORNING: The Mission of the Church and the Function of Personal Evangelism

1. Lecture (30 minutes) using charts and Scripture relating to "light, salt, and yeast." Key concept is "penetration." Our job is to come and to take—come to Christ; take him to our friends.
2. Discussion groups (75 minutes)
   • What is our group doing in personal evangelism?
   • What could we be doing that we aren't?
   • How could we put our plans into action?

SATURDAY EVENING: The Message of the Church

1. Lecture (30 minutes) with charts, developing an evangelistic life-style. What do we talk about when we witness (love, confession, repentance, forgiveness, peace, joy, hope—Bible verses for each)? Point out excuses often given by people for not becoming a Christian.
2. Discussion groups (60 minutes). Each group is divided into threes. One plays the role of a non-Christian and others try to convince that person to become a Christian. This process should lead to conversion of youth who come without previous commitment to Christ. (When this plan was used, three decisions were made.)

SUNDAY WORSHIP

1. The Joy of Witnessing (15 minutes). List and demonstrate the use of about ten basic Scriptures for personal evangelism.
2. Communion Service (20 minutes). The youth bake special bread for the occasion. Youth come forward as they want to, in groups no larger than fifteen.

40 FOCUS: ELECTRIC CHRISTIANITY
Bob Dent

1. What is communication? Use on arrival a barrage of religious and secular music, followed by discussion with reference to Marshall McLuhan's *The Medium Is the Massage,* and also use several nonverbal communication games.
2. What are values? See *Faith/at/Work,* February, 1972, and *Psychology Today,* April, 1970. Use a values questionnaire (could use ideas from *Values Clarification* by Sidney Simon). *Assignment:* Tape commercials and collect ads.
3. What values does the world communicate to us? How effective are commercials/ads in communicating values? Share collections and discuss them. (If possible, collect old TV commercials from a TV station.)
4. How and what is the church communicating? Using tape recorders, have youth interview people on the street: how they feel about church, and what they think the church is saying to their community. Play back the results. *Assign* each person a different section of Luke to study in preparation for discussion suggested in paragraph 5.
5. What do we want to share with the world about Christ? Use nonverbal trust games. In groups of four share and study assigned passages. Have the groups list some things they want to share about Christ. Have the groups decide to what human needs the particular Good News they have isolated is being addressed. Select one or two ideas which they feel might be developed into radio spots.
6. Look at what some groups have done with radio/TV spots professionally in sharing Christ. Contact Ms. Lois Anderson, Broadcasting and Film, 475 Riverside Dr., Rm. 852, New York, NY 10027.
7. Communicating the GOODS NEWS ELECTRICALLY.

Have groups finish writing their spots. Record locally or at a radio station. Stations will often accept a 20-second public service spot for no charge. *Assignment:* Study Acts: What do we want to share about the church? How can we use the media to communicate community electrically?

RESOURCES: Luke/Acts; Marshall McLuhan, *The Medium Is the Massage;* Lyman Coleman, Serendipity books; Dennis Benson, *Electric Evangelism.*

41   MARATHON RESOURCE MATERIALS

THEME OUTLINE

I. TRUST IN GROUP

A. Private questionnaire:
1. Do the members of the group care about each other? never/sometimes/always
2. Do YOU care about others in the group? never/sometimes/always
3. Do you feel that the members of the group care about YOU?
4. Do you need the group? How? Now or in the future?
5. Does the group need you? How?

B. Introduction to group discussion/exercises:
1. Frustration—with group: exercise—paper/balloons (wad/throw/pop)
2. On floor—relaxing/deep breathing: fantasy trip through own body
3. Circle trust
4. Dyads/discussion. List things turned on about group/turned off by it. Introduction to group of your partner in dyad.
5. "Open/closed" group? Why? How? Breaking in/out of circle?
6. Name three people in group with whom you are most similar. Name three whom you would like to become more like. Discussion.
7. Line up people (including leaders) in the order of who has shared himself/herself most honestly with the group. When finished, place yourself. Questions/discussion.
   (Instead of moving actual people, because of the high threat level and time involved in a large group, you might use the names of people on cards and have them move the cards.)
8. Look at group LEADERSHIP: broomstick exercise. Have four or six people hold onto a broomstick. Instructions: do anything you want with it *without talking* to each other. Rest of group is instructed "to watch." Let exercise go on at least 4 minutes. Will be "slow" starting probably. Stick may break (high tension/conflict level!).
   Reflect on: "How did you feel holding the stick?"
   "Who was making the decisions?"
   How is this exercise related to our group life?

II. TRUST IN SELF (following above, watch for appropriate times for breaks)

A. Make a collage representing yourself. Hang. Have group sharing.
B. Personal reflection: Do you trust yourself:
   —to make decisions about values, goals, actions?
   —to share your feelings (all kinds)?
   —to deal with your own feelings and those of others?
   —to depend on others? (*Exercise:* give a person a pencil or other small object. Put it in shirt pocket. Tell person to "get it out without using hands, any way he/she can." Will stand on head, etc. Few will ask someone else to take it out for them. *Exercise:* trust fall.)
   —to depend on self; stand alone; with God?
   —to solve problems?
C. Exercise: strength bombardment.

III. TRUST IN GOD

A. Exercise: charades (two people choose each stance and must enact it.)

   Atlas—carries the world on shoulder; feels the whole burden of life.
   Sysiphus—keeps rolling the stone up the hill even though it will roll right back down; futile effort/knows it/keeps on "truckin'."
   Apathy—nothing's worth believing or doing; zilch.
   Pie in sky by and by—suffer now, but get reward later; accept things as they are because in the end, in another world, justice will be done.
   Head—enjoy yourself now; turn on to something; forget the world: (playboy philosophy, drugs, alcohol, etc.) hedonistic.
   Human—human nature is perfectible—at least it is the ultimate! We can change and if we work for it, we will have a bigger and better, more just and loving world for all.
   Arty—God is everywhere: reverence for all of life. Spend time learning, appreciating, and expressing beauty and truth of life (through media/music, writing, art, meditation, etc.)

Courage—accepts that which cannot be changed; works to change that which can be changed for justice and love to reign among all; seeks wisdom, resources; trusts in God to know the difference.

B. Questions/Discussion:

1. Are any of the above Christian? Why? Why not?

2. Who is a Christian? A person who:
   — has certain *beliefs* about God?
   — does certain *actions* in the name of God?
   — makes decisions in a *certain* way following God?
   — has certain *experiences* from God, with God?
   — makes a decision to follow Jesus, the Christ, and live his style of life?

3. Why be a Christian? Who is God? What is God?
   Where is God?
   How does God make himself known in the world?
   Have you ever felt God?
   Give opportunity for commitment,

4. Exercise:
   a. Paint a collage to show how you've felt God's love; to show how you've shared God's love.
   b. Make a group creation based on Scripture.

C. Overview: What is love? Tie self, group, and God together.

CREATE a picture of the relationship between SELF-GROUP-GOD.

SUNDAY WORSHIP

(All the various exercises listed in the sections of the marathon were *NOT* completed *during the night. Several* were incorporated into the worship experience.)

(Held a 3½ *hour service* by choice of the group. Had several opportunities to stop—Spirit was moving.)

1. *Singing*
2. *Collage painting*—show how you have felt God's love. Sharing, discussion.
   Listening: George Harrison's "Hear Me, Lord" from "All Things Must Pass" album.
3. *Scripture study*—rewrite passage or story in contemporary setting or portray the story in movement/drama or through some other medium (a group activity: 10 or so in a group).
   a. Job

b. Proverbs 3:5 and 6 ("trust in the Lord with all your heart. . . .")

c. Romans 8 (different gifts of the Spirit) (or Ephesians 4)

4. *Action/discussion* of group's presentations. Many different group abilities and individual abilities, God given, are to be used in his service.

5. *Strength bombardment*—one at a time—30-second sharing of positive qualities of each person.

6. Old Testament concept of COVENANT:
   a. history—meaning of term—presentation.
   b. *US* developing a Covenant: Listing what we as a GROUP will promise each other/God when we return home.
   c. Forgiveness aspect of covenant:
      WHAT DO WE need to be forgiven for?
      LISTEN: George Harrison: "Forgive Me, Lord, Please."
      One word or sentence sharing of what we need to be forgiven for. . . . "Prayer" introduction to this sharing—group AND GOD.
   d. NEW START—power of Jesus' Spirit / resurrection / OLD GROUP DIES / NEW GROUP BORN. (PAINFUL, AS WE HAVE FELT.)

7. *Prayer / Singing / Silence / AMEN.*

(During the silence, a "wind" came through the windows and "lifted" the bottom edges of the covenant papers off the wall; there was NO other breeze felt during the WHOLE day. The group felt this as another evidence of the Spirit's presence; it was remembered for years!)

42 CLARIFYING OUR CHURCH INVOLVEMENT
Laneita Dunphy and Bernie Linnartz

I. A LOOK AT MY CHURCH INVOLVEMENT

A. List the activities that you see the church offering.

B. List the activities that you would LIKE to see the church offer.

C. Using the two lists, place—

   A by those activities you do alone, *P* with people.

   $ by those that are strictly monetary involvement.

   + by those that happen only in church.

   F by those which have a free, sharing, open atmosphere.

   O by those which allow minimal or no participant response.

   * by those which invite all ages to participate.

U by those where you feel uncomfortable; C by those where you feel the opposite.

I by those where you contribute time, effort, and personal involvement.

E by those you consider in-depth encounter.

B by those activities you consider busy work.

D by those you consider your duty as a member.

R by those you feel are shallow and repetitious.

S by Sunday only activities.

G by those from which you have received most growth.

T by those which are ends in themselves.

CO by those which have carry-over in the growth of your faith.

L by those directly related to everyday living.

II. WHAT I NEED

A. With List A, choose five activities that are of most importance to you. Rank them 1–5. List the needs that are met for you in each.

B. With List B, choose five activities that are of most importance. Rank them 1–5. List needs and/or interests you have in each activity. Compare lists and see in what way(s) the present church activities are or are not meeting your needs.

III. ON BELONGING TO THE CHURCH (Rank your feelings)

A. The church

___ provides people with the values they should have to lead a Christian life.

___ works with people to assist them in clarifying their own values.

___ supplements the values given to us by family.

___ provides biblical interpretation to understand values in life.

B. My joining the church was

___ a "single intense, inspirational" experience.

___ the result of search and study.

___ to please someone else.

___ the result of societal expectations—"good to belong."

___ a very positive involvement with people who are members of the church.

___ family tradition.

IV. TOWARD CLARIFYING MY FAITH

A. My faith in God is: (Locate your position on the scale of 1-10 for each.)

clear confused
1   5   10

remains unchanged   shows considerable growth
1   5   10

B. Rank items below as YOU feel about them. You may choose not to rank certain items which do not pertain to you.

1. I feel my strongest faith is in: ___ God, ___ self, ___ others, ___ Christ as found in people.

2. My faith comes from: ___ seeing Christ in people ___ an in-depth religious experience; ___ a calm, continuous search and study; ___ a significant relationship with another person; ___ the Bible ___ a special calling that I feel I have received; ___ encouragement from my parents.

3. My present faith is: ___ an up-and-down experience; ___ a continuing search and study; ___ a strong, steady belief; ___ uncertain; ___ a "crutch"; ___ an uplifting, happy feeling; ___ other. List.

43 PLANNING CONFERENCE
First Baptist Church,
San Bruno, California
Ron Brushwyler

FRIDAY:

6:00 P.M.—Leave for conference site.

8:00–10:00 P.M.—General Session #1:
Songs, Introduction, Worship.
Presentation: "First Baptist: Security and Mission in Conflict."
Role Playing:
1. The church concerned with SURVIVAL.
2. The church concerned with MISSION.
4 x 4 buzz groups.
Feedback and major proposals; formation of small study groups on the mission of the church.

SATURDAY:
8:00—Breakfast.
8:45–10:00— Board/committee meeting #1: Discussion of the strategy study report.
10:15–11:45—Board/committee meeting #2:

Discussion of "Preface to Parish Renewal."

1:00– 3:30—Board/committee meeting #3: Formulation of programs for next program year. (See following questions.)

4:00– 5:45—General Session #2. Master calendar coordination; closing worship.

6:00—Dinner.

6:30—Leave for home.

Resources for use: Board/Committee Meeting #3

1. What are the major objectives of First Baptist Church?
2. What are the basic strengths of our program?
3. List our most important accomplishments last year.
4. How can we maintain these strengths and accomplishments in the coming year?
5. Where is our program in basic need of improvement? (Think in terms of your board or committee's area of responsibility.)
6. How can these improvements be categorized? (*a*) Those that can be met immediately; (*b*) those which should be achieved this year; (*c*) those which should be accomplished within two years; (*d*) those requiring more than two years to achieve.
7. What are the major obstacles in the way of achieving these basic improvements?
8. What specific steps would you be willing to take to accomplish basic needed improvements in our church program?
9. Considering improvements needed, who can we enlist to assist us in accomplishing these needs?
10. What specific dates/programs need to be put on the church calendar and formulated?

44   PROGRAM PLANNING RETREAT
Redford Nash

This retreat uses a planning process to get at the assumptions/givens about the group.

FIRST SESSION: Airing things out.

1. List three likes and three dislikes.
2. What would I change and create?
3. Can I think of myself as a planner? Plan a vacation for ten days, using $400. Decide where to go, what to do. Estimate the cost of lodging, transportation, meals, recreation. Develop an itinerary. Share the plans—the participants will *prove* they can plan!
4. Ask people to work in pairs with each area of group planning—recreation, study topics, excursions, parties, retreats—and to develop a *minimum* of one page of ideas.

SECOND SESSION:

1. Each pair shares the list of ideas, and copies of the list are circulated to all in the group.
2. All in the group are given the number of excursions/retreats for the quarter, and each is told to design an ideal program for the quarter (or other period of time) using the ideas already generated.

THIRD SESSION:

1. Individuals share their creations and proposed calendar.
2. The group chooses the best of the creations.
3. The group develops a consensus of the items to include on the master calendar.
4. The group develops a way to present the program to the larger group.

Specific goals are assumed in this process of planning for study, recreation, excursions/retreats. In this planning process, no time is given to developing goals as such. Program units are created within the existing goal structure. (One assumed goal is the involvement of youth in the planning of their own program.)

45   BOARD OF CHRISTIAN EDUCATION RETREAT
(Hatboro Baptist Church)

FRIDAY:

8:00—Arrival, social hour, sharing.

SATURDAY:

7:30—Children eat.

8:00—Adults eat.

10:30—Discussion period: job descriptions.
Teens: serious film, discussion.
Children: play, Bible story, refreshments.

12:00—Lunch for all.

1:00—Worship; discussion and personal evaluations.
Teens: free.
Children: outdoor recreation/games.

3:00—All free time (parents responsible).

5:30—Dinner

6:30—Discussion: Board priorities for next year.
Teens and children: fun films and games.

8:00—ALL families together: singing, family games, closing thoughts, sharing.

SUNDAY:

10:00—Worship: Families together: special worship-oriented activities BY FAMILY. Joint sharing, celebration.

11:00—Meditation hour.

12:00—Coffee, donuts.

12:30—Free recreation time.

2:00—Dinner.

3:30—Discussion, evaluation.

The following sheet for personal reflection was distributed to the participants before the retreat.

Sheet for reflection BEFORE the retreat:

AREAS FOR CONSIDERATION:

In each area/category consider:

A. If you could have your IDEAL, how would you like the group (or individual) to function?

B. How would you evaluate the past? Consider feelings about what has/hasn't happened; strengths and weaknesses.

C. What changes would you recommend: general, organizational, in job descriptions, etc.?

Personal: In the next six months to one year how would I like to see myself change? My family? My relationship to God?

General Board:

A. Board of Education: organization, function, and philosophy. (A., B., C.—see above.)

B. Communication within the church: between boards, and with other groups (association, and the total community). (A., B., C.—see above.)

C. Unity of purpose, function between Sunday church school and the total church program.

Specific Board Job Descriptions: (A., B., C.—for each, 1-10)

1. leadership education; recruitment training and morale.

2. nursery/children, I and II.

3. youth.

4. adults.

5. publicity/missions.

6. chairman.

7. secretary.

8. audiovisuals.

9. library.

10. pastors.

The reflection sheets were used as the basic material for sharing of needs, goal setting, deciding priorities, evaluating the past, planning specifics, and eventually writing new job descriptions for ALL board of Christian education positions.

46 LEADERSHIP WORKBOOK FOR CHRISTIAN EDUCATION IN THE BLACK CHURCH
(Prepared by Milton Owens, based on July/August, 1971, issue of *Spectrum*—summarized.)

PURPOSE: To provide guidance for black pastors and lay leaders to evaluate their Christian education program and to consider new directions for their educational ministries. (Lamentations 3:40; 2 Corinthians 3:5)

PROCEDURE:

1. Pastor and key leaders read July/August issue of *Spectrum,* 1971.

2. Series of sermons.

3. Pastor and key leaders from ALL church boards plan five sessions (2½ hours each) of leadership training in Christian education. (Worship, small-group work, and sharing being part of each session.)

SESSION I: Examine Your Community—Part I.

(Background reading: *Spectrum,* articles beginning on pages 19 and 22.)

1. Describe your community. In small groups or pairs tour a 10-block area surrounding the church. Visit shops, agencies, etc., even bars. Observe; converse with people. Return to church after one hour and discuss the experience in relation to items *a–e.*

   a. socioeconomic (income) level of people.

   b. physical condition of houses/businesses.

   c. educational/social services in the community.

   d. community attitudes toward the church.

   e. community political involvement/awareness.

SESSION II: Examine Your Community—Part II.

1. Read Matthew 5:38-48. Interpret in your own words.

2. Review your findings from the community tour. List:

   a. three most important issues/problems facing the community.

   b. three most important concerns for children.

   c. three most important concerns for youth.

   d. three most important concerns for adults.

SESSION III: Defining Mission

(Background reading: *Spectrum,* articles beginning on pages 10, 14, 5.)

Goal: to define the mission of your church in terms of what you have discovered about your community and the gospel (working in groups of five).

1. Read Mark 16:15 and Matthew 23:23-24. List the three most important things your church is currently doing.

2. Review the following (one at a time) and indicate how your church is, could, or should respond to:

   a. three critical issues facing the community.

   b. three important concerns for children.

   c. three important concerns for youth.

   d. three important concerns for adults.

3. Based upon the total data you have collected thus far, indicate the three most crucial concerns or issues.

4. Define the mission of your church in terms of your community and the gospel.

SESSION IV: Examine Your Teaching Ministry

(Background reading: *Spectrum,* articles beginning on pages 25, 28, 33, 41.)

Study the following Scriptures and examine your church's educational ministry in light of them: Matthew 23:2-7; 23:13-15; Mark 16:15; Acts 17:1-15; Exodus 18:13-24; and Exodus 24–26.

SESSION V: Developing Educational Experiences

(Background reading: *Spectrum,* articles beginning on pages 33, 41, 44, 47.)

1. Review/evaluate all the information you have collected. Does this information describe the persons in your auxiliaries, church school, and other programs?

2. What have you learned or relearned in these studies?

3. Practice brainstorming by finding five uses for a brick other than its customary use in building. *Now brainstorm ideas for educational* experiences using all the information/data/needs you have gathered in the previous sessions.

4. Use your list to make choices and to plan specific *new* educational experiences related to the mission of your church.

   (See Appendixes 1 and 6.)

The complete *Workbook* is available from Milton Owens, American Baptist Churches, Valley Forge, PA 19481. Enclose $1.00 to cover the cost of postage and copying.

47 LEADERSHIP TRAINING WORKSHOP
(Greenville Baptist Church, Rhode Island)
Ethel Stickney

Day included use of the following to rank/discuss the most important "Characteristics of a Christian Leader."

In small groups work exactly 20 minutes ranking the sixteen statements in the order that *the group* feels would be the most significant characteristic of a Christian leader. You are to work as a group, in any way you like, making decisions as a group. Rank the highest as 1.

1. Possesses empathy/compassion toward others.
2. Is able to interpret his faith to others.
3. Attends church regularly.
4. Bases his life on faith in Jesus Christ as Lord.
5. Has strong desire to help the weak and downtrodden; has deep concern for social justice.
6. Is a tither.
7. Seeks to be a reconciler wherever he is.
8. Lives with a clear conscience.
9. Seeks to win people to Christ.
10. Trusts God even when things go wrong.
11. Is able to love those who do not respond to him.
12. Sees his church work as the means to heaven.
13. Reads the Bible daily; engages in private devotion.
14. Is committed to the church as the group especially called to serve the world.
15. Is not judgmental of others.
16. Has hope in eternal life.

48 A WORKSHOP ON PRAYER
Sister Carolyn Campbell

Selected elements from five sessions (total of 1½ days):

1. Scripture study: Matthew 6:1-20 (Christ alone); Luke 11:1-13 (temptation); John 17 (prayer).

2. Each group (of 3) created a poster expressing the meaning of one sentence of the Lord's Prayer.

3. Presentation/alone time on "Why pray?" Each person was given another's name to pray for. Each person was given stationery and asked to "describe hearing Jesus speak to you" to a friend who has never heard of Jesus.

4. Focus on the temptation of Christ and his agony in the Garden. Use discordant electronic tape/silence/J. Collins' "Amazing Grace"/group prayer.

5. Planning session.

Each participant was given a resource booklet: "ABC's of Prayer" which included short quotes from: Pierre Teilhard de Chardin, Bishop C. Bardsley, and others.

49   OUR M-T AND M-D QUOTIENTS
(M = Mini, Midi, Maxi; T = Thinking;
D = Doing)
(Used with adults)
Ted and Jean Taylor

FRIDAY:
9–10:30 P.M.—Candlelight Forum:
Thinking Quotient
"What I Believe and Why"
Moderator and four panelists
SATURDAY:
9:30-10:30 A.M.—The Action Scene:

Doing Quotient
Panel of moderator and four persons making short presentations on the international situation, crime prevention, social action, transportation, and environment.

10:45—Mini discussion session
2:00– 6:00—Free for M communion with nature-/friends. Mini, Midi, Maxi hikes
7:30– 9:00—Maxi activity—square/folk dancing
Midi activity—moonlight stroll
Mini activity—conversation on bridge
9:30—Campfire, singing, wiener roast
SUNDAY:
10:00 A.M.—Worship service/Evaluation
(Price ranges from $31.25 to $40.00 per person.)

50   CHANGE: PROMISE OR THREAT
(Adult retreat)
Ted and Jean Taylor

FRIDAY: (one-hour segments after dinner)
1. Introduction and social hour
2. Candlelight forum: "How I Have Changed"; moderator and three panelists
3. Group discussion with forum speakers
SATURDAY:
9:30–10:15 A.M.—Keynote address and talkback: "The Impact of Change"
10:30–12:00— Small-group discussion: "Changes That Are Needed"
2:00–3:00— Action Panel and discussion: "What I Would Like to Change" moderator and three panelists
7:30–9:30— Group activities: games, skits, campfire singing, wiener roast
SUNDAY: Worship Service

51   CELEBRATIONS OF LIFE AND DEATH
Ron Keeshan

Used in study and in contemporary worship over a 9-month period.
BOOKS: People are encouraged to buy and read:
1. *On Death and Dying,* Elisabeth Kübler-Ross
2. *Modern Vision of Death,* N. Scott
3. *Death Education: Preparation for Living,* Betty Green and Donald Irish.

RESOURCES IN WORSHIP:
1. Film: *The Highest Bidder* (Paulist, Insight film); *Between the Cup and the Lip* (Mass Media Ministries); *To Die Today,* Elisabeth Kübler-Ross.
2. Selections from: C. Wertenbaker, *60 days in a Lifetime.* Leroy G. Augenstein, *Come, Let Us Play God.*
3. Drama: "To Hell with Aunt Agatha," in Norman Habel's *What Shall We Do with All These Rotting Fish?* and "The Time My Father Died," by J. Matthew.
4. "Barrington Bunny," from *The Way of the Wolf,* by Martin Bell.
5. W. Knight, "Song of Our Syrian Guest"—variation of Twenty-third Psalm. Used in Communion with anointing foreheads with olive oil.

52   "A DAY APART": WOMEN'S PRAYER/MEDITATION RETREAT
Fern Allison

8:00—Arrive at Scout camp; worship, songs, other music.
8:30—Bible study (Romans, sections; also use large cartoons from *How to Be a Christian Without Being Religious,* by Fritz Ridenour).
9:30—Worship God: in quiet times and in hustle/bustle.
10:00—Play Corrie ten Boom's taped testimony. Have brief discussion of her suggestions/introduction to resource booklet for the day.
10:45—Alone time for meditation/crafts.
11:45—Lunch
12:15—Afternoon worship
12:30—Bible study
1:30—Discussion of Catherine Marshall's suggestions—from *Beyond Our Selves.*

1:45—Quiet time/meditation
2:40—Sharing time
3:00—On way home

Each woman was given a resource pamphlet including Corrie ten Boom's suggestions (found at the back of her book, *The Hiding Place),* quotations from Catherine Marshall, and space for personal reflection, writing, and comments.

53   DEACONS' RETREAT
Dean Dolash

DAY OF DISCIPLINE: 7 A.M.–4:30 P.M.—Began with light breakfast.

Three brief breaks; noon was a fast, with options for nonfasters; Communion closing.

GOALS: 1. unity as a board;
2. training in spiritual growth methods:

METHODS: 1. searching the Scriptures
2. praying
3. hearing taped messages and gospel music
4. talking/sharing with one another
5. silent meditation

Bible passages studied in silence and with a workbook included: Romans 15 and John 6 (15 min. each). Six subject areas were studied. In each area, the pastor (P) read several selections, each man (M) read additional selections to himself, and was then asked to write down for himself what "God said to me. . . ."

The Bible:
(P) 2 Timothy 2:15
1 Thessalonians 1:5; 2:13
1 Peter 3:2
(M) Joshua 1:7-8
Psalm 1:1-3

God's Promises
(P) 2 Corinthians 1:19-20
John 16:23-24
Romans 4:20-21
(M) John 14:12-14
Ephesians 3:20-21

Stewardship:
(P) Luke 6:38
(M) 2 Corinthians 9:6-15

Obedience:
(P) 1 Samuel 15:22
Hebrews 5:8
Jeremiah 7:23
2 Corinthians 10:3-6
(M) Romans 2:1-11
James 1:21-23

Prayer:
(P) Matthew 7:7-11
Matthew 26:36-46
Luke 18:1-8
(M) Matthew 17:1-21
James 5:16
1 Thessalonians 5:17-19

God's Gifts:
(P) 2 Corinthians 9:15; Ephesians 1:3; 1 Corinthians 2:11-12; 2 Peter 1:2-3. (M) 1 Corinthians 1:4-9.

Additional readings were included by the leader, from: *The Knowledge of the Holy,* by A. W. Tozer; *How to Be Filled with the Spirit,* booklet and tape from Campus Crusade for Christ.

List of Resources for Retreats

(For those who are just starting to collect resource materials, we have selected some materials for suggested purchase. The FIRST STRING ¹ can all be purchased for under $40. Once you have those and have had a chance to use them, you will be in a better position to choose further. The SECOND STRING ² selections can all be purchased for under $45. (All prices are subject to change.)

GENERAL PHILOSOPHY
(Working with people/youth/retreats):

1 1. John L. Carroll and Keith L. Ignatius, *Youth Ministry: Sunday, Monday, and Every Day.* Valley Forge: Judson Press, 1972. $1.65. Basic philosophy, organizational procedures, planning.

1 2. Martha M. Leypoldt, *Learning Is Change.* Valley Forge: Judson Press, 1971. $2.95. Written about adults but applicable to youth. Good basic philosophy of change process and a great section on evaluation.

3. Merton Strommen, *Five Cries of Youth.* New York: Harper & Row, Publishers. $6.95. Survey of 7,000 youths within the church. They share their cries of loneliness, outrage, family crises, closed minds, and joy.

4. Muriel James, *Born to Love* (TA for churches). Reading, Mass.: Addison-Wesley Publishing Co. $5.95. Application of transactional analysis to church situation; useful tools in understanding communication problems and skills. For TA training, write to ITAA, 3155 College Ave., Berkeley, CA 94705.

5. Gerald and Elisabeth Jud, *Training in the Art of Loving: Local Churches and the Human Potential Movement.* Philadelphia: United Church Press, 1972. $7.95. Philosophy, research, and details of three-day "shalom" retreats (at Kirkridge Retreat Center, Bangor, Pennsylvania) which blend the ancient Christian witness and new methods of group encounter and sharing.

6. Nancy Geyer and Shirley Noll, *Team Building in Church Groups.* Valley Forge: Judson Press, 1970. $1. Materials, procedures, outlines of team-building sessions.

7. Thomas Gordon, *Parent Effectiveness Training.* New York: Peter H. Wyden, 1970. $6.95.

8. Andrew Weil, *The Natural Mind: A New Way of Looking at Drugs and the Higher Consciousness.* Boston: Houghton Mifflin Co., 1972. $2.95. Excellent book on motivations for drug use and its relation to theology.

GROUP-BUILDING BASICS
(Exercises, awareness processes):

1. J. William Pfeiffer and John E. Jones, eds., *Handbook of Structured Experiences for Human Relations Training.* La Jolla, Calif.: University Associates, 1973-74. $5.00 each. Box 80637, San Diego, CA 92138. Vols 1, ¹ 2, ² and 3.² Complete instructions for group exercises, games. Write to University Associates for schedule of training events. **1 2**

2. Sidney Simon et al, *Values Clarification.* New York: Hart Publishing Co., 1972. $3.95. Over 60 actual instruments (check sheets, questions, group exercises, games) for use in clarifying values with individuals and groups. For workshops in value clarification, write to AM HEC, Springfield Road, Upper Jay, NY 12987. **1**

3. Lyman Coleman, *Serendipity* Series. Waco, Tex.: Creative Resources, Word, Inc. Serendipity sampler, $1. Suggested starting books: youth—*Rap,* or general book—*Celebration.* Twelve books in the series. Coleman also leads over 30 one-day workshops in major cities in the U.S.A. Write for a schedule. **1**

THEMATIC ISSUES AND PROGRAM MATERIALS:

1. *Respond* Series. Vols. 1, 2, 3, 4. Valley Forge: Judson Press. Contains materials created and used by youth and leaders all over the U.S.A.

2. Dennis Benson, *Recycle Catalogue.* Nashville: Abingdon Press. $6.95. Over 700 creative ideas for learning, fellowship, mission, and celebration. Created, tested, and proven at the very grass roots by folk like you and me.

3. David Thornton, *Faith Recycling.* Valley Forge: Judson Press. $1.50. A process for understanding your personal beliefs.

4. Discovery Series. Paramus, N.J.: Paulist Newman Press. Especially fine are *Discovery in Word, Discovery in Prayer,* and *Discovery in Song.* Prayers, quotes, etc., organized by theme areas.

5. Concern Series. Silver Burdett, Morristown, NJ 07960. Student books, 60¢ each; leader's guide for whole series, $1.95.

6. Argus Choose Life Series. Write for catalog of books and materials to 3505 N. Ashland Ave., Chicago, IL 60657.

7. Ann Billups. *Discussion Starters for Youth Groups,* series 1, 2, and 3. Valley Forge: Judson Press.

8. Martin Bell, *The Way of the Wolf: the Gospel in New Images.* New York: Seabury Press, Inc. $4.95.

9. Kenneth Koch, *Wishes, Lies and Dreams: Teaching Children to Write Poetry.* New York: Random House, Inc., 1971. $1.95.

GENERAL PERIODICALS:

1. *Recycle,* ed. Dennis Benson. Box 12811, Pittsburgh, PA 15241. $5 for 9 issues. Also, *SCAN,* same address. $6 per year.

2. *Strategy.* 1132 Witherspoon Bldg., Philadelphia, PA 19107. Bimonthly. $5.50 per year. Presbyterian youth workers' publication; good articles, resources, and in 1974 a series on retreats.

3. *Faith/at/Work.* Box 1790, Waco, TX 76703. Bimonthly. $5 per year. Articles: church renewal, personal and group spiritual growth, ideas for groups, etc. Write for workshop and conference schedule.

4. *The Wittenburg Door,* ed. Denny Rydberg. Youth Specialties, 861 Sixth Ave., Suite 411, San Diego, CA 92101. Bimonthly, $10 per year. Write for workshop and conference schedule.

DEVOTIONAL MATERIALS, WORSHIP RELATED, SELF-DISCOVERY, SPIRITUAL GROWTH:

1. Norman C. Habel, *Interrobang.* Philadelphia: Fortress Press, 1969. $1.95. Book of litanies, prayers, poems, tools for celebration written by high school youth. Also, Norman C. Habel, *For Mature Adults Only.* Philadelphia: Fortress Press, 1969. $1.95. Youth expressions about failure, death, sex, fear, truth, faith and love—poetry/song; and Norman C. Habel, *Wait a Minute, Moses.* St. Louis: Concordia Publishing House, 1965. $1.25. A look at youth, freedom, bondage, and Moses.

2. David J. Randolph, ed., *Ventures in Worship,* vol. 3. Nashville: Abingdon Press, 1973. $3.95. Creative experimental worship materials; excellent annotated bibliography.

3. Malcolm Boyd, *Free to Live, Free to Die; Malcolm Boyd's Book of Days; Are You Running with Me, Jesus?*—all three: Signet NAL paperbacks, 95¢ each. Prayers, reflections for meditation, worship, programs.

4. Ruth and Arthayer Sanborn, *Do You Hear Me, God?* Valley Forge: Judson Press, 1968. $1.95. Book of prayers, reflections.

5. Michel Quoist, *Prayers.* New York: Sheed & Ward, Inc., 1974. $5.95. Contemporary prayers.

6. John Brown, *New Ways in Worship for Youth.* Valley Forge: Judson Press, 1969. $3.75. Resources for 20 worship services.

7. Grady Nutt, *Being Me.* Nashville: Broadman Press. $1.75. Program and worship material around the theme: "I am a person of worth created in the image of God to relate and to live."

8. H. Victor Kane, *Devotions for Dieters.* Valley Forge: Judson Press, 1967. $2.50.

9. Paul S. McElroy, ed., *Prayers and Graces of Thanksgiving.* Mount Vernon, N.Y.: Peter Pauper Press, 1967. $1.25.

10. Fritz Pawelzik, *I Lie on My Mat and Pray.* New York: Friendship Press, 1964. $1.50. Also, Fritz Pawelzik, *I Sing Your Praise All the Day Long.* New York: Friendship Press, 1967. $1.50. Prayers by young Africans.

11. Herman C. Ahrens, Jr., ed., *Tune In.* Philadelphia: United Church Press, 1968. $2.95. Prayers by youth, from *Youth* magazine.

SCRIPTURE TRANSLATIONS:

1. Clarence Jordan, *Cotton Patch Version of Matthew and John* (1970); *Cotton Patch Version of Luke and Acts* (1969); *Cotton Patch Version of Paul's Epistles* (1968). New York: Association Press. Each $4.50. Contemporary Scripture translations in a southern Georgia setting.

HUMOR:

1. Charles Schulz, all Charlie Brown, Peanuts, series of paperbacks. Fawcett Crest books. 50¢ to 95¢ each. 15 books. Check your used books bookstore.

2. Vernard Eller, *The Mad Morality: Or the Ten Commandments Revisited.* Nashville: Abingdon Press, 1970. $2.79. Also, Robert L. Short, illus., *The Gospel According to Peanuts.* New York: Bantam Books, Inc., 1970. 75¢. Paperback. Use of cartoons theologically.

3. "B.C.," "Wizard of Id," and "Wee Pals." Each in paperback series. New York: Fawcett World Library,

Gold Medal Books. 60¢ to 75¢ each.

4. "Mad" paperback series. New York: Signet imprint of New American Library, Inc., 60¢ to 75¢ each.

5. Shelley Berman, *Cleans and Dirtys*. Los Angeles: Price, Stern, Sloan, Pubs., Inc., 1964. $2.50.

6. David Evans, *The Good Book*. Los Angeles: Price, Stern, Sloan, Pubs., Inc., 1972. $2.00. Humorous cartoons based on New Testament incidents.

GENERAL:

1. Peter L. Steinke, *Right, Wrong, or What?* St. Louis: Concordia Publishing House, 1970, Concordia Perspective No. 10. $1.25. Frank sharing of teens (ages 15 to 20) about their feelings/views about sex.

2. T., W., and M. Moore, *Sex, Sex, Sex*. Philadelphia: United Church Press, 1969. $1.95. Solid content, guaranteed to be picked up and read.

3. Arlo Tatum and Joseph S. Tuchinsky, *Guide to the Draft*. Boston: Beacon Press, Inc., 1969. $2.45; and Allan Blackman, *Face to Face with Your Draft Board*. Chicago: World Without War Publications, 1972. $1.25. Both are excellent. The selective service system is still functioning.

4. Edward Steichen, ed., *Thé Family of Man*. New York: The New American Library, 1967. $2.95. Black and white pictorial history of the family of man.

5. Gene Sharp. *Exploring Nonviolent Alternatives*. Boston: Porter Sargent, Inc., 1971. $2.25. National defense systems built from nonviolent strategies.

6. Haim Ginott, *Between Parent and Teenager*. New York: Avon Books, 1973. $1.50. Good material for discussion reflection.

7. Keith Miller, *A Taste of New Wine*. New York: Bantam Books, Inc., 1973. $1.25; and Keith Miller, *A Second Touch*. Waco, Tex.: Word, Inc., 1972. $1.25. Personal growth and renewal in the church.

SIMULATION GAMES/GAMES:

1. Dennis Benson, *Gaming*. Nashville: Abingdon Press, 1971. $5.95. Book and two records. Includes six games AND teaches you how to create your own simulation games.

2. Donald E. Miller et al., *Using Biblical Simulations*. Valley Forge: Judson Press, 1973. Volumes 1 and 2 (1975), $4.95 and $5.95 each. Biblical simulation games for use with church groups.

3. World Wide Games. Box 450, Delaware, OH 43015. Write for catalog.

4. Ideas Series. Vols. 1-15. $5.95 each. Youth Specialties, 861 Sixth Ave., Suite 411, San Diego, CA 92101.

Published quarterly; each volume organized by sections. Try volume 8 if you have not seen the series.

MUSIC (Hymnbooks, sheet music):

1. *Songs.* Yohann Anderson, Box 722, Novato, CA 94947. $1.75. Words and chords for over 300 songs, both religious and "secular." (Spiral-bound volume and cassettes also available.)

2. Catalog from Proclamation Productions, Inc., 7 Kingston Ave., Port Jervis, NY 12771. (Many books $1 each: *Hymns Hot and Carols Cool; Hurrah for God; Alive and Sing; Songs for the Easter People.*)

3. *Sing 'n' Celebrate*. Word, Inc., Waco, TX 76703.

4. *Hymnal for Young Christians*. Vols. 1 and 2. F.E.L. Publications, Ltd., 1925 Pontius Ave., Los Angeles, CA 90025.

5. *Here Comes the Son*, Maranatha Songbook. Maranatha Publications, P.O. Box 954, Santa Cruz, CA 95060. $1.00 each.

OTHER MEDIA:

1. RECORDS: See appendix of David J. Randolph, ed., *Ventures in Worship*, Vol. 3. Nashville: Abingdon Press, 1973. $3.95.

2. DRAMA:

   a. *Plays for the Church*, NCC Council Press, Dept. of Church and Culture of the Division of Christian Life and Mission, 475 Riverside Drive, New York, NY 10027.

   b. Albert Johnson, *Best Church Plays*. Gloucester, Mass.: Peter Smith. $6.00.

   c. Norman C. Habel, ed., *What Are We Going to Do with All These Rotting Fish?* and Seven Other Short Plays for Church and Community. Open Series No. 4. Philadelphia: Fortress Press. $2.95. Short plays which raise religious themes/questions.

3. FILMS:

   a. Films heavily used by youth/church groups:

Adventures of an*	*Neighbors*
The Golden Fish	*The Rink*
Orange and Blue	*The Wall*
A Child's Eyes:	*Phoebe*
November 22, 1963	*The Game*
An Occurrence at Owl	*The Merry Go Round*
Creek Bridge	
The Hat	*The Most*
The Hole	*One Friday*
The Hand	*The Stray*
Hangman	*Lord of the Flies*
Happy Birthday, Felisa	*The Sun Seekers*
Memorandum	*Parable*
	It's About This
Have I Told You Lately	*Carpenter*
That I Love You?	*The Detached*
A Chairy Tale	*Americans*
The Daisy	*The Interview*

The Apple
Satan's Choice
Zuckerkandl
Homo Homini
Two Men and a
    Wardrobe
Clay
Leaf
Sky
Run!
The Great American
    Funeral

Death of a Peasant
Get Wet
Black & White
Sky Capers

Johnny Appleseed
The Smile
The Toymaker
The Magician
American
    Time Capsule
Is It Always
    Right to Be
    Right?

Time Out of
    War
The Preacher
The Nail
Frank Film
Acceleration

 b. Sources (a starting list):
  1. Mass Media Ministries, 2116 N. Charles St., Baltimore, MD 21218.
  2. Contemporary/McGraw-Hill Films, Princeton Rd., Hightstown, NJ 08520.
  3. National Film Board of Canada, Suite 819, 680 Fifth Avenue, New York, NY 10019.
  4. Pyramid Films, Box 1048, Santa Monica, CA 90406. For a complete listing of all sources and many films (reviewed), see *Audio-Visual Resource Guide,* Ninth Edition, New York: Friendship Press. $8.95.

1 4. SLIDEMAKING (Media shows, use in Bible study/worship):

 a. Ed McNulty, *How to Do It Handbook: Gimmicks, Gadgets and Grace* (80 pp. mimeo.) Order from him at 2999 Bethel Church Road, Bethel Park, PA 15102. $4 includes postage. Theological basis for media in church, and "how-to" for church groups.
 b. Media supplies: If you can't find locally, write to

Griggs Ed. Service, Box 362, Livermore, CA 94550 for catalog and list of materials.
 c. Media Source-book. San Francisco Theological Seminary. $3.50. Detailed information/resources for those who are planning to use media in community ministry: radio, TV, cable TV.
 d. Lyman Coleman and Ken Curtis, *Festival.* A Serendipity book. Waco, Tex.: Creative Resources, Word, Inc., 1973. $3.95. Making your own movies as a group.

CRAFT RESOURCES:

 1. How to tie-dye: PO Box 307, Coventry, CT 06238. Free.
 2. Miss Rit, Consumer Service Dept., 1437 W. Morris St., Indianapolis, IN 46206. "Dye Craft" and "A Leader's Guide to Dye Craft"—free.
 3. Dona Z. Meilach, *Contemporary Batik and Tie-Dye.* New York: Crown Publishers, Inc., 1972. $4.95.
 4. Anne Maile, *Tie-and-Dye as a Present-Day Craft.* New York: Taplinger Publishing Co., Inc., 1963. $6.95.
 5. In leather work, we had great luck with TANDY, a national chain with stores all over the U.S.A., which helped us figure out what *not* to buy. Gave leaders two hours of free instruction. *Very* cooperative and helpful. Kits out on consignment. For catalog and list of all stores in U.S.A., write TANDY, Box 791, Ft. Worth, TX 76101.

TRAINING OPPORTUNITIES:

 For training opportunities contact the denominational headquarters of your church. Also, see the references included with many of the books and pamphlets in this List of Resources.

List of Contributors

1. Fern Allison, 11 Court St., Yreka, California.
2. Joel Bjerkestrand, Associate Pastor, King of Glory Lutheran Church, 1171 E. Bell De Mar, Tempe, Arizona.
3. Betsy Bouska, United Methodist Youth Council, Grinnell, Iowa.
4. Rev. Mason L. Brown, Minister of Christian Education, First Baptist Church, Kansas City, Missouri.
5. Rev. L. Ronald Brushwyler, First Baptist Church, San Bruno, California.
6. Sister Carolyn Campbell, Community of the Transfiguration, Cincinnati, Ohio.
7. Bob Dent, Central Presbyterian Church, Chambersburg, Pennsylvania.
8. Rev. Larry Dobson, First Baptist Church, Trenton, New Jersey.
9. Rev. Dean Dolash, First Baptist Church, 7th and Harrison St., Charleston, Illinois.
10. Rev. Robert Dougherty, Pastor, Danville Baptist Church, Danville, California.
11. Rev. Brent Dugan, Fairmount, West Virginia.
12. Dennis C. Evans, Director of Church Activities, National Baptist Memorial Church, 16th St. & Columbia Rd., Washington, D.C.
13. First Presbyterian Church, Parkersburg, West Virginia.
14. Jim Foster, Christian Counseling and Teaching Center, Charlottesville, Virginia.
15. Joe Haren, First National Bank, Canton, Ohio.
16. Rev. Gary Jenkins, West Hills Christian Church, 999 Thorn Run Rd., Coraopolis, Pennsylvania.
17. Rev. Alvin D. Johnson and Ethel Stickney (Administrative Assistant), Greenville Baptist Church, Greenville, Rhode Island.
18. Ron Keeshan, Santa Fe, New Mexico.
19. Rev. Bernie Linnartz, Westminster Presbyterian Church, 533 S. Walnut St., Springfield, Illinois.
20. Redford B. Nash, First Presbyterian Church, 2001 El Camino Rd., Oceanside, California.
21. Glenn Oswald, 1419 State Rd. 29, #20, Phoenixville, Pennsylvania; worked with J. Junke and Dallas Lutheran Youth in Dallas, Texas.
22. Rev. Milton E. Owens, Board of Educational Ministries, American Baptist Churches, Valley Forge, Pennsylvania.
23. Rev. Timothy Peterson, ABC Campus Minister, 1740 Illinois St., Fort Wayne, Indiana.
24. Rev. Arlo Reichter, Associate Minister, First Baptist Church, Los Angeles, California.
25. Rev. Harold Schock, resource person to youth, First Baptist, Yakima, Washington; now on mission service in Hong Kong.
26. Bill Tallent, Don Baird, and Senior High Youth, Vine St. Christian Church, Nashville, Tennessee.
27. Ted and Jean Taylor, Helen and Victor Coles, Unitarian Church of Arlington, Virginia.
28. Rev. Revis E. Turner, Minister of Christian Education and Youth, First Baptist, Lima, Ohio.
29. Rev. Larry K. Waltz, Associate Executive Minister, Philadelphia Baptist Association, Philadelphia, Pennsylvania.

PLANNING/PROBLEM SOLVING	EVANGELISM
Ask some people to be observers for the small groups given tasks of relating the meaning of a Scripture passage; ask them to observe who plays what role in blocking or facilitating the accomplishment of the task and the development of group closeness.	Have groups or individuals make taped, or visual, or written news announcements, commercials, ads, etc., of biblical truths. Submit to local radio and TV stations and local papers or publish your own. Share them with other churches and organizations. Scripture Readings: Matthew 5:38-48—love enemies; Matthew 23:23-24—intent of the Law; Mark 16:15—the Great Commission; Acts 17:1-15—Paul evangelizing (22).
Scripture: Lamentations 3:40; 2 Corinthians 3:5, expressing need to evaluate. Exodus 18:13-26, about decision making	Hold worship service in public place—beach, street, park, etc. Invite others to join you. Dialogue sermon, drama, and music are particularly effective at drawing attention and expressing a message. Have individuals available to talk with people who come and have questions.
Covenant with one other person or in small group to work on a selected problem-solving task; plan target date and ways to follow up with one another.	Prepare a statement or letter in affirmation of your faith to be shared with one other person (at least) upon your return home. Develop a group-faith symbol for posters, buttons, silk-screened onto T-shirts, etc., to be visible to the world. Create a "Back-Home Bag" with reminders of the retreat to share with others. Slides, movies, and tape recordings are especially fine discussion starters and lures.

Bright-colored stickers (sold in stationery stores) can be used in a greeting activity with people writing greetings and sticking them on one another. (Stamps or masking tape can also be used.)

Have free time for settling in; then have a meal together. For example, on a Friday evening have a 1 A.M. Brunch and Sing. (24)

Using an inner circle and an outer circle with an equal number of people in each and moving in opposite directions, assign a task appropriate to the level of closeness in group. Strangers could find likenesses (e.g., birth dates, shoe size, kind of toothpaste); people more acquainted could do nonverbal eye contact or share a feeling about a theme or person. (26)

Divide into small groups for orientation, introducing self (name and something special); state purpose of group, role of leaders, expectations of retreaters; go over schedule; discuss questions; start theme. (24).

Rope-Tie Mixer: After listing name and birth date of each person in room, find the person whose name is listed opposite the number closest to your date of birth; get a length of rope to tie your forearms together by a certain time. (26) Variations: use a long rope; use other common features.

Group Mirroring: In groups of two, one leads in motions, the other follows; then in fours, eights, etc. Music accompaniment. (19)

GROUP BUILDERS

Adopt a group mascot or symbol (for example, lions on party stickers, patches).

Watch for group symbols to emerge as a reminder of the place, event, the meaning. Could be a song, slogan, etc. Means to celebrate and share.

Ask people to bring and share their favorite thing.

Involve everyone in altering your environment—cleanup, murals, plastic hemispheres, balloons, setting up tents, beautifying, etc.

Develop drama or chant impromptu around a word, a prop, or a feeling (in small groups).

Recreation: all kinds of team sports, tug-of-war, keep-away with large ball, Nerf balls, play with a parachute, capture-the-flag, tobogganing, water balloons, a rain hike, some table games.

GROUPS OF FAMILIES

Use communication worksheets (Appendixes 13 and 14).

Have each person or each family unit make a family coat of arms (see Sidney Simon, et al., *Values Clarification).*

In family groups, have everyone contribute to creating a skit, mobile, or collage around the theme or Scripture. Bring a grab bag full of crafts and props.

Using stimulus of taped or recorded portion of a TV show about family (e.g., "All in the Family," "The Waltons," "The Brady Bunch"); discuss in family units or two families together similarities and differences in patterns of relating, values, ways of handling discipline, etc.

*(Numbers refer to List of Contributors)

BIBLE STUDY

A group of three is given one line of a biblical passage to create a poster or banner expressing that line. Other lines are given to other groups of three. The creations are then shared with the larger group, making the whole passage in visual symbols. Passages readily used in this way: Lord's Prayer, Sermon on the Mount. Variation: mural.

In small group, update Scripture lesson to modern times in writing, role play, drama, or craft.

Sing Scripture! Many psalms and passages are set to music.

Use a Scripture passage as a responsive reading.

WORSHIP

Hold hands in a circle while praying conversationally; everyone who wishes offers sentence prayers.

Guide group prayer, leader suggesting theme, others praying around this focus. Several focuses may be suggested, one after another.

Celebration with music and balloons. Have many balloons to be blown up by participants. While music plays, everyone enjoys trying to keep balloons off the floor, fellowshipping in the bumping and cooperation. (19)

Move to "Bridge Over Troubled Water": some people forming bridges with their arms and backs, others crossing over and under; ending in a large circle. Nonverbal.

Develop a group litany, starting each line with a phrase like: "Yes, we are. . . ." Thank God for. . . ." "God gives his people. . . ." Spontaneous.

Feast of Fools' Celebration: Based on ideas from Transactional Analysis and Harvey Cox. Have people bring fruit or homemade bread; cheese and meat provided. Banners and posters on walls, helium balloons, interest centers, everyone in costume. Enjoy feast of food and appearances. Then everyone participates in activity of interest center: singing, folk dancing, banner and box-collage making, mural and finger painting. Share creations. Have Communion and slides and music. (Contributed from folks in Chicago)

Treat the whole meal as Communion; introduce with Scripture; have music and meditation while eating. Prepare foods likely to have been eaten in Jesus' time.

Each bring something from environment or activity of the retreat and offer it with a word expressing your faith to God, placing it on a table, at the fireside, etc.

Fit together contributions from workshops to make a participatory worship service; e.g., arts, drama, dance music, media, writings, readings.

CLOSINGS

In circle share spontaneous thoughts, questions, songs, prayers, evaluation.

Meet in total group to reflect. Break into groups of two: (1) recall from the beginning of retreat to now; (2) ask, "What are some insights that are real to you?" Individually do group-gram—reflect about it. Again divide in twos: (1) ask, "Has group-gram changed?" (2) apply theme to home/school/church; (3) role-play a relevant situation. Individually fill out evaluation sheets. (19)

Ask individuals to write down their expectations of the retreat; share in small groups; post on the walls. Leaders show how they are being or not being taken into account.

Brainstorm by using letters of the alphabet to stimulate new words or thoughts.

Have people make a collage defining the issue: for example, "What the Church Is" collage. (17)

4 x 4 Wishing Game: (1) If I could take off for a month and money were no problem, I would like to go to. . . . (2) If I could take one friend (outside my family) who has meant a lot to me, I would invite—— because. . . . (3) While on a trip, I would like to goof off a few days doing. . . . (4) The greatest thing I would like to have happen during the planning conference is. . . . (Do these in groups of fours.)   (5)

Use badges, buttons, stickers, armbands, or signs to share your faith with people while traveling to retreat, at rest stops, and with others sharing the retreat facilities.

Ask small groups to plan an element during the retreat: e.g., impromptu game, special way for serving the meal, etc.

In an atmosphere of candlelight, introduce the challenge of expanding friendship and of "sentencing to death" any unhealthy conflicts or barriers existing between self and others in the group. Then in silence write on paper two things: my biggest obstacle in relating to others in this room, and that in relating with Jesus Christ. In a ceremony, symbolize the release of these obstacles by burning in the candle flame the papers naming the obstacles. (26)

Go to the person with whom you have communicated least. Talk with each other about (1) why you chose each other; (2) the position you feel in the group. Share some past experiences of communicating that were important to you.

Explore giving, receiving, and losing love. Sing together "They'll Know We Are Christians by Our Love." Read 1 John 4:7-11. Play the Love Gifts' game (J. William Pfeiffer and John E. Jones, eds., *Handbook of Structured Experiences for Human Relation Training* (SEHRT), vol. 1, p. 113). Have the winners of the game plan an original way to show their love to the others. (20)

WOOD-YOU: Gather pieces of wood in center of the circle; have each person find a piece of wood to give to another person. Negotiate pieces chosen by more than one person. Tell why you are giving the wood to that person. Allow time to see what people do with their gifts and how long it takes to give and receive. Feedback. (19)

PROGRAM IDEAS CHART*

PERSONAL GROWTH

Have interest centers for self-expression, such as:

music	stickers
painting (finger,	sculpture (clay,
fluorescent, etc.)	pipe cleaners)
banner making	graffiti board (19)
collages (mural, boxes)	tapes & recorder
movement to music	reading & writing
puppetry	table games
shrink-art	sing-along
handprints	

For a group which is acquainted: each person says a word to each other person, selecting words which recognize that person's need, gift, or talent. (9)

Emotional unpacking: share in small group some concern left behind, or what your day was like before coming.

Tillicum (Indian word meaning "secret friend")
1. Upon arrival, each writes own name on popsicle stick; names are drawn from hat and kept secret.
2. During retreat, each is to be a special friend to the person whose name he/she has drawn.
3. At the end of retreat, each tries to guess his or her *Tillicum*. Everyone shares the truth. Very affirming to individuals. (15)

Variations of *Tillicum:* (1) Secret partner is called Christkin. (2) Pairing may be done by drawing names, but not kept secret. The pairs then become prayer partners during the retreat, meeting several times for prayer and sharing.

Upon arrival have each person make a handprint, footprint, or self-collage. Hang these around room. During the retreat, group members write upon the hangings positive characteristics of that person. At the end of retreat, have small-group strength bombardments as each print or collage is returned to the owner.

"Who Am I?" theme: Serendipity groups to help share past and present. Visual presentation on "Why Am I Afraid to Tell You Who I Am?" Small-group creation of skits based on *games people play* at home, church, school. Review and discuss TV commercials focusing on the pressures of the world on ME. Use the Beatitudes of Jesus to compare our life-style to Christ's. View and discuss film *Baptism.* Set guidelines for our life goals. (11)

CONCEPTUAL GROWTH

Have participants as individuals or small groups make buttons, badges, banners, collages, or stickers related to the theme.

Ask people to dig into pockets and purses to find something related to theme. Share in twos; then fours, or eights "right now I. . . ." (4)

Planners create an atmosphere by music, candles, visuals related to theme; people experience mood as they arrive.

Get your theme by brainstorming. Set the tone for ideas popping without criticism. See list of theme ideas in Appendix 11.

Ask small groups to develop for the rest of the group an exercise or presentation related to the theme.

Use one of the following films related to interpersonal relations for discussion starters: *A Chairy Tale, The Hat, Neighbors, The Rink, It's About This Carpenter.*

Use plays or readings to develop understanding of community building: "Like Ships in the Night"; *What Shall We Do with All These Rotting Fish?;* "A Fairy Tale" by Claude Steiner; *Interrobang; For Mature Adults Only.* (See List of Resources)

PERSONAL GROWTH	CONCEPTUAL GROWTH
Prepare a personal Bible study-guide booklet. Include questions to guide learning and to apply to passages, and give instructions about silence and timing. (9) Paraphrase Scripture in own words. Make a collage or craft project relating the meaning of Scripture passage. Overviews: Have people write "The Bible—My Version" or ask, "If the Bible were blank, how much could you 'put back'? Which portion of the Bible do you live?"	Paraphrase or write letter or role-play the viewpoints of various persons in scriptural times from your passage. Make available a concordance, Bible dictionaries, commentaries, and atlases for people to answer "who, what, when, why, how" questions about passage.
Silent prayer or meditation accompanied by sacred music. Print up and give out suggestions for meditation. Have Scripture and symbolic action relating to footwashing to preface going forward to Communion table which is centered in room and has on it symbols of events of retreat. As ready, each goes forward to kneel, break bread, and dip in juice. May invite friend. Music hummed or sung. Theme of darkness and light. Darkness and noise increasingly drown out Scripture being read (John 1:1-4). Then with flashlights and candles, light grows as worship progresses with Scripture, song, slides, and movies of contrasts *(Newsreel of Events of 1968,* Castle Films), and interpretive movement. Songs used: "Sounds of Silence," "Who Will Answer?" "The True Light," "Lord of the Dance," "You Are the Light of the World," "Shalom." Scripture: John 1:1-17, Psalm 150; Isaiah 9:2-7; Matthew 13:10-16; Luke 6:46-49. (13) **"Renewal of Vision" theme:** Vision of God: Read Isaiah 6:1-8, Jeremiah 9:23, 24. Now practice. Vision of God's World: Psalm 24; John 3:14-17; reading from M. Quoist, "Practice Being Aware." A Vision of My Purpose: Trust—Romans 3:23-26; Follow—Matthew 4:18, 19; Worship—Philippians 2:5-11; Discover His Will—Romans 12:1-2; Be a Servant—John 13:3-17. Read "The Brick," by M. Quoist. (10)	With music and slides, present collage of our world and its meaning. Tape contemporary musical groups which are making an impact on our culture. Show Pepsi commercials to taped music, including voice of Martin Luther King in "I Have a Dream," the Celebrates, "Three Day Night," sound from Woodstock, "We Shall Overcome," and "Peaceful Children." (19) 1001 Bits of Life: each person writes on colored pieces of paper aspects of life to celebrate. Put up around the room. Music in background. (19) "Image of Jesus" theme: Listen to and compare secular hymns about Jesus, such as Ocean, "Put Your Hand in the Hand" George Harrison, "My Sweet Lord" "Choose Life" theme: Film *Adventures of an**—animated, theme of seeing and being saved. Relate the song "Both Sides Now," by Judy Collins, to the gospel. *Newsreel of Events of 1968:* Castle Films. (13)
In twos, request one another, "Help me write a letter to myself about what I feel right now that I will want to remember on March 1 next year." What goals, commitments, concerns? Address envelope and seal it—to be kept unopened until that date.	Write or share in twos statements of new learnings gained. What was relearned?